The
Etiquette of
Freemasonry

The Etiquette of Freemasonry

A Handbook for the Brethren

by
An Old Past Master

Skyhorse Publishing

PUBLISHER'S NOTE TO THE THIRD EDITION

THERE are two matters treated in this work—viz.: ' Hearty Good Wishes,' p. 164, and Opening and Closing (in full) a Board of I.Ms., p. 264—which may be open to discussion ; but it has been thought well to leave them here just as they were handled by our late esteemed, venerable, and expert Bro., who very carefully revised the Second Edition.

CONTENTS.

CHAPTER V.

THE PERFECT EQUIPMENT OF A LODGE.

CHAPTER VI.

DRESS, JEWELS, AND PUNCTUAL ATTENDANCE.

CHAPTER VII.

THE TYLER AND HIS MULTIFARIOUS DUTIES.

CHAPTER VIII.

THE PREPARATION OF CANDIDATES AND THE K......S.

CHAPTER IX.

DIVERSITIES IN THE OPENINGS AND CLOSINGS.

CHAPTER X.

THE CHAPLAIN AND HIS DUTIES.

CHAPTER XI.

OBSERVANCES IN THE OPENINGS.

CHAPTER XII.

OBSERVANCES IN THE CLOSINGS.

CHAPTER XIII.

RETROSPECTIVE, AND AS TO NUMBER OF CANDIDATES AT ONE TIME.

CHAPTER XIV.

INITIATION OF A CANDIDATE.

CHAPTER XV.

INITIATION OF A CANDIDATE (CONTINUED).

CHAPTER XVI.

THE SECOND DEGREE.

CHAPTER XVII.

THE THIRD DEGREE.

CHAPTER XVIII.

MODE OF SALUTING, AND OTHER MATTERS.

CHAPTER XXII.

SPEECHES AND THE CHARITIES.

CHAPTER XXIII.

PUBLIC CEREMONIALS, INCLUDING THE FUNERAL SERVICE.

PAGE

E—Preparation in the First Degree.

F.—Poor Letter 'H.'

G.—The Charge in the First Degree.

H.—Explanation of the Working Tools.

L.—The Installation Ceremony.

THE ETIQUETTE OF FREEMASONRY.

CHAPTER I.

INTRODUCTION ; SCOPE OF THE WORK.

Explanation of the Title—On the Manner of performing the respective Duties of the Lodge—For whom the Book is intended—The Minor Jurisprudence of the Craft—The Author's Masonic Career — Importance of the Office of Director of Ceremonies—Correction of Palpable Errors—Misquotations from the Bible—Misstatements of Historical or Biblical Events, etc.

IN introducing this treatise upon the Etiquette of Freemasonry to the attention of the members of the Craft, it is desirable that a brief explanation should be given of the title selected for the work.

The word 'Etiquette' is intended to be understood, not only in its general—although somewhat restricted—signification, namely, 'The social observances required by good-breeding,' but also in its wider and more comprehensive meaning, as 'Regulations as to behaviour, dress, etc., to be observed by particular persons upon particular occasions : forms which are observed in particular places' (Dr. Ogilvie's Dictionary).

In accordance with this wide interpretation of the word ' Etiquette,' many duties and details not provided for in the Book of Constitutions, or in any Ritual extant, will be fully considered, and, where necessary, will be discussed and explained in this work.   It is also intended that the means and appliances, the technicalities and ceremonial observances, as distinct from the verbal portions of the Ceremonies, which are indispensably necessary for the decorous and harmonious working of the business of the Lodge, will be detailed, and, where it may be needful, will be fully explained.

It will readily be conceded that, in addition to the words of the several Ceremonies, there is need for instruction in *the manner* in which the Officers of the Lodge should perform certain portions of their respective duties.   The Rituals contain directions here and there, but they are necessarily brief, and in some cases they may be misunderstood or wrongly interpreted.   The saying is trite, but strictly true, that the Master of a Lodge—be he never so perfect himself—can do little unless he be well supported and assisted by his Officers ; whereas, if he be intelligently and zealously assisted by them, and the Ceremonies be well rendered by all concerned, the resultant effect upon the Candidate—almost to a certainty—will be, that he will form so favourable an opinion of the Institution, as to inspire him with a lasting love of the Craft, such as will cause him to become—in fact, and not in name only—' a true and faithful brother among us.'

On the other hand, if the duties of the subordinate

Officers be performed in a perfunctory or slovenly manner, the beauty and the impressiveness of the several Ceremonies will be materially marred or altogether lost, so far as their effect upon the Candidate is concerned.

The experience of every thoughtful and intelligent Freemason, who attends his own Lodge with tolerable regularity, or who occasionally visits other Lodges, will fully confirm this assertion. He must have known instances wherein the want of attention to details, on the part of certain of the Officers, and the absence of the necessary preparation for the business to be transacted, have led to confusion and delay, and have in a great measure marred the effect of the Ceremonies. At a critical moment, in some important part of the Ceremony, which may have been led up to by a probably serious address, something—indispensable to the continuity of the work—is not at hand; it may be the alms-dish, or the apron with which the Candidate in either degree is to be invested, or the heavy M... in the Third Degree, or some other equally important detail.

In cases such as those mentioned, a certain degree of confusion is inevitable; there are whisperings, and hurried messages, and dartings hither and thither, to the great annoyance of all concerned, and to the certain distraction of the attention of the Candidate.

This work is commended to the attention of Officers of Lodges, of aspirants to office, and of all Freemasons who are lovers of order, in the earnest hope that the irregularities and inconveniences hereinbefore mentioned may, as far as is possible, be guarded against in their several Lodges.

It will be seen from the title-page of this work, that one of its objects is to discuss 'the minor jurisprudence of the Craft.' Jurisprudence is defined as 'the knowledge of the laws, customs, and rights of men in a state or a community.' As far as we, as a community, are concerned, the Book of Constitutions may be taken as containing the major jurisprudence of the Order ; but, upon the principle of 'de minimis non curat lex,' there are numberless small, but far from unimportant matters not considered in the Constitutions, which form part of our system, and to which it is desirable to call attention in a work of this character, dealing, as it is intended to do, with all the details, great and small, in any way connected with the Lodge, the Ceremonies, and the general business of the Craft, as far as private Lodges are concerned.

There is in every state and community the 'lex non scripta,' which, from precedent and immemorial usage, is held to be of equal force with statute law. Of this character are many of our ancient customs, upon which our Constitutions are silent.

Having thus sketched in outline the objects and the intentions of this work, the author trusts that he will not lay himself open to the charge of egotism if—in order to show that he possesses one necessary qualification for the task which he has undertaken, namely, a long and an exceptionally varied experience of Freemasonry in different parts of England—he gives, as briefly as possible, an account of his Masonic career.

He was initiated in a Lodge near London in March,

1841. After passing through several of the lower offices, he was installed as Worshipful Master of a very important Lodge (not his mother-Lodge) in 1846.

From the time of his first taking office in 1843, to the present time, he has, with few and brief intervals (caused by changes of residence), either been in office or has taken a more or less active part in the working of the Ceremonies in the various Lodges in different Provinces, of which he has from time to time been a member.

He has been the Master three several years of different Lodges. He is a Past Prov. Gr. Deacon of one Province, a Past Prov. Gr. Registrar of another, and a Past Prov. Gr. Senior Warden of a third. In addition to these, he has during four consecutive years filled the office of Prov. Gr. Third Principal in the Royal Arch Degree.

One office which he has filled in two different Lodges is that of Director of Ceremonies. He has for several years held that office in the Lodge of which he is now a member, and by the blessing of T.G.A.O.T.U. he retains it, after more than sixty years of work in the various Lodges of which he has been a member in the past.

The foregoing brief sketch of the author's Masonic life is given with a twofold object. Firstly, as he has premised, in order to show that he has an amount of authority to speak, and to, at least, endeavour to instruct his younger brethren, such as an unusually long and active experience may be supposed to confer ; and, secondly, because he wishes, as having himself long served the office of Director of Ceremonies, to impress upon his readers the great importance and the general usefulness of that office, if the many duties thereof be zealously and energetically performed.

A Director of Ceremonies is far too often omitted from the list of the Officers of a Lodge, or when such an Officer is appointed, it not unfrequently happens that some junior member is selected for the position— one, possibly, quite young in the Craft, and necessarily with little experience of the practical working of the Ceremonies, and of the ' Etiquette ' of the Order.

The following extract from a recently published work, 'The Revised Ritual of the Craft,' published by A. Lewis (see Appendix A, page 236), will show how multifarious and how really important the duties of a Director of Ceremonies are.   The address is delivered at the investiture of the brother who is appointed to the Office, on the day of the Installation of the Worshipful Master.

DIRECTOR OF CEREMONIES.

Bro. ......, I have the pleasure of investing you as Director of Ceremonies. Your Jewel, the Cross Staves, is the emblem of power and authority.   It will be your duty to see that everything be done decently and in order, and that there be no confusion or mismanagement in the Ceremonies, or other business of the Lodge.   You will be expected to see that the Lodge-room is properly prepared for all Masonic meetings ; to receive visitors, and to assign to them their places in accordance with their rank in the Craft ; to marshal all processions and demonstrations of the Brethren, both within and without the Lodge, and to give the honours at Masonic festivals. In addition to these, your regular duties, you will be expected to render assistance (when needed) to the Deacons and other Officers, and generally to see that the Ceremonies are decorously and correctly conducted. In order that you may be duly qualified for the performance of these multifarious duties, I would recommend to you a diligent and careful study of the practical working of the Ceremonies, as well as with the ancient usages and the established customs of the Fraternity, in order that you may with due authority correct that which may be wrong, and while *encouraging* and *directing enlightened and progressive improvement,* you may guard against unconstitutional ' innovations in the body of Freemasonry.'*

The foregoing definition of the duties of a Director of Ceremonies will show clearly that no mere tyro in the Craft 'is sufficient for these things.' The important functions which he has to discharge, both in the Lodge and in the banquet-room, require that he should be a man of long and varied experience in Freemasonry, and that he should have filled the greater number of the offices in the Lodge ; in short, that he should be a master of the Etiquette of Free-

---

* If practicable, it is better for a Past Master to fill the office of Director of Ceremonies. He is qualified by a more lengthened experience to *direct* the proceedings (subject always to the W. M.) ; and his dicta upon points of procedure and other matters will come with the authority which experience gives. In the event of a P. M. being invested as D. C., some portions of the address should be omitted.

masonry in its widest sense, and be fully qualified 'to correct, to guide, and to instruct his brethren.'

In the following chapters, while discussing the Ceremonies of the three Degrees in whole or in part, it may be necessary to allude to, and even in some cases to introduce, portions of the Ritual. These will be given for the sake of illustration only, and they will be as few in number and as brief as may be consistent with a clear explanation of the meaning intended to be conveyed ; or if they are occasionally enlarged upon, it will be in order to correct palpable errors, and to suggest a possibly better way in form or phraseology.

Some misquotations from the Bible, or misstatements of historical or Biblical events, will be mentioned, due regard and reverence being always shown for all that may, with justice, be entitled to be called Landmarks of the Order.

CHAPTER II.

THE APPELLATION OF THE ORDER.

Masonry or Freemasonry ?—Masons or Freemasons ?—Operative and Speculative Masonry—A Notable Fact proved—Antiquity of the Order—Freemasonry the only Correct Term—Illustrative Anecdote—Discrepancies.

IT will be convenient in this place, and it will be not altogether foreign to our subject, to discuss, as briefly as we may, the appellation of the Order of which we are members. Is it 'Masonry' or 'Freemasonry'? Are we 'Masons' or 'Freemasons'? The following excerpts from the 'Lecture in the First Degree' furnish a conclusive reply. An old 'Manual of Freemasonry' runs thus :

INTRODUCTORY ADDRESS.

Brethren, Masonry, according to the general acceptation of the term, is an Art founded on the principles of Geometry, and directed to the service and convenience of mankind. But Freemasonry, embracing a wider range, and having a more noble object in view, namely, the cultivation and improvement of the human mind, may with more propriety be called a Science.

In the recently published Ritual, to which allusion is made in the previous chapter, the introduction runs thus :

First Section.

Brethren, *Masonry*, according to the general acceptation of the term, that is, operative, practical masonry, is an Art founded upon the principles of Geometry, and is directed to the use and the service of mankind, in so far only as their physical and material needs and comforts and convenience are concerned. *Freemasonry, on the contrary*, being purely speculative, and having higher aims, and embracing a wider range, namely, the cultivation of the moral virtues, and the general instruction and improvement of the minds of its members, may with strictest propriety be denominated a Science. In accordance, however, with the immemorial custom of the Order, its lessons generally are veiled in Allegory, and are illustrated by an appropriate and expressive system of Symbols.

To draw aside this mingled veil of Allegory and Symbolism, and to penetrate more deeply into our Mysteries than the ordinary routine work of the Lodge enables us to do, is the object and intent of our Masonic Lectures, and it is only by a careful and diligent study of those Lectures that we can hope to become acquainted with the true interpretation of our Symbols, and to gain (in some measure) a clear knowledge and understanding of our more recondite Mysteries.

The seventh section of the first Lecture commences thus, in the older Rituals :

Q. Brother Senior Warden, Masonry passing under

two denominations, viz., Operative, and Free and Accepted, to which of these do you belong?

A. To the Free and Accepted.

Q. What is learned from Operative Masonry?

A. The useful rules in Architecture, whence an edifice derives figure, strength, and beauty, and bears a due proportion and an equal correspondence in all its parts.

In the Revised Ritual, the phraseology is slightly different but the meaning is the same:

Seventh Section.

Q. Brother Senior Warden, in the short address which I delivered at the commencement of this Lecture, I clearly defined Operative or practical Masonry, as distinguished from Free and Accepted or speculative Masonry. I will now ask you, in the first place, what is learned from Operative Masonry?

A. The useful rules in Architecture, from which an edifice derives figure, strength, and beauty, and maintains a due proportion and an equal correspondence in all its parts.

Q. What do you learn by being a Free and Accepted Mason?

A. Secrecy, Morality, and Good Fellowship.

Q. What do you learn in the Lodge?

A. To act upon the Square; to pay a proper and becoming respect to the Worshipful Master and his Wardens; and to abstain—while in the Lodge—from every topic of religious or political discussion which might breed dissension among the Brethren, and might possibly entail scandal upon the Craft.

In the foregoing quotations, the distinction drawn between Operative or practical Masonry, on the one hand, and purely speculative Freemasonry on the other, is clear, emphatic, and unmistakable.

The following sentences, taken from a brief sketch, entitled 'Freemasonry ; its Origin, History and Design,' which forms the introduction to a manual of the Ceremonies of Craft Masonry, are very clear upon the subject of the appellation of the Craft. In this extract one notable fact is incontestably proved, *proved up to the hilt*—namely, that from the earliest formation of the Guild the members thereof called themselves distinctly *Freemasons, not Masons*. (The Italics used in the extracts are not in the original) :

'The descendants of the Roman colleges of artificers established schools of architecture, and taught and practised the art of building among the newly enfranchised people. . . . From this school of Lombardian builders proceeded that society of architects *who were known at that time by the appellation of Freemasons*, and who from the tenth to the sixteenth century traversed the Continent of Europe, engaged almost exclusively in the construction of religious edifices, such as cathedrals, churches, and monasteries. The monastic orders formed an alliance with them, so that the convents frequently became their domiciles, and they instructed the monks in the secret principles of their art. The Popes took them under their protection, granted them charters of monoply as ecclesiastical architects, and invested them with many important and exclusive privileges. Dissevering the ties which bound them tò the monks, these *Freemasons* (*so called to distinguish them from the rough masons*, who were of an inferior grade, and not members of the corporation) subsequently established the guilds of stonemasons, which existed until the end of the seventeenth century in Germany, France, England, and Scotland.

'These stonemasons, or, *as they continued to call themselves, Freemasons*, had one peculiarity in their organization which is necessary to be considered if we would comprehend the relation that exists between them and the *Freemasons* of the present day. The society was necessarily an operative one, whose members were actually engaged in the manual labour of building, as well as in the more intellectual occupation of architectural designing. This, with the fact of their previous connection with the monks, who probably projected the plans which the Masons carried into execution, led to the admission among them of persons who were not operative Masons. These were high ecclesiastics, wealthy nobles, and men of science who were encouragers and patrons of the art. These, not competent to engage in the labour of building, were supposed to confine themselves to philosophic speculations on the principles of the art, and to symbolizing or spiritualizing its labours and its implements. Hence there resulted a division of the membership of the brotherhood into two classes, the practical and theoretic, or, as they are more commonly called, the operative and speculative, or " *domatic* " and "*geomatic.*" The operative Masons always held the ascendancy in numbers until the seventeenth century, but the speculative Masons exerted a greater influence by their higher culture, their wealth, and their social position.

' In time, there came a total and permanent disseverance of the two elements. At the beginning of the eighteenth century, there were several Lodges in England, but for a long time there had been no meeting of a great assembly. In the year 1717, *Freemasonry* was revived, and the Grand Lodge of England was established by four of the Lodges which then existed in London. This revival took place through the influence and by the exertions of non-operative or speculative Masons, and the Institution has ever since mainly preserved that character. . . .

' *Freemasonry* of the present day is a philosophic or speculative science, derived from, and issuing out of, an operative art. It is a science of symbolism.'

In the foregoing excerpts, from the very thoughtful, and doubtless historically correct, sketch of the early period of which it treats, showing as it does the continuity of our Order, by lineal descent, from a remote antiquity, two facts stand clearly revealed : Firstly, that during some centuries previously to the year 1717, the higher Order of the builders or architects '*continued* to call themselves *Freemasons.*' (The word ' continued ' is very important.) And, secondly, that after the reconstitution of the Order in 1717, the Operative element was eliminated, at once and for ever ; and our Craft became in reality that which it had been for centuries in name—*Freemasonry.*

Hence we may fairly insist that the use of the words 'Masons' and 'Masonry,' whether in the Lodge or in Masonic publications, is clearly contrary to historical precedent, and tends to debase our ancient and noble Order, by lowering it from a speculative Science to a mechanical art, trade, or business.

Every Freemason who is zealous in the service of the Craft, and who is tenacious of its honour and prestige, should by every means in his power urge the discontinuance of an appellation to which, under no circumstances, can any honour, or grace, or dignity be attached.

The attention of the writer of these pages was many years ago peculiarly and forcibly directed to this subject in the following manner : He was suffering from a rather serious derangement of a vital organ ; his medical adviser wished him to consult a specialist. Speaking of this to another medical man, who was a Freemason, the latter said : 'I will give you a letter of introduction to Dr. Bence-Jones, whom I know intimately.' The letter was handed to the doctor as soon as the writer was admitted ; after reading it, and making inquiries as to symptoms, etc., the doctor said : 'I cannot understand how you can have got into this bad state of health ; your occupation is a healthy one—it must give you a great amount of out-of-door exercise.' 'No,' was the reply ; 'my occupation is a sedentary one—it involves many hours indoors every day.' 'Why,' said the doctor, 'Dr. P. B. says' (reading from the letter) 'the bearer is not a patient of my own—I know him well as a *Mason*.' Dr. Bence-Jones took this to mean a *stonemason* and *builder.* He laughed heartily at the mistake, as did afterwards the writer of the letter of introduction. The latter, however, from that day forward, never failed to use the correct term, Freemason.

One would naturally suppose that the erudite Brother who wrote the historical sketch from which the long extract is given on pages 26-28, would have perceived that the word 'Mason,' as applied to a member of the Craft, is a misnomer; yet in the very Manual to which that sketch is an introduction we find in the 'Opening of the Lodge in the First Degree' the following : 'W. M.—Bro. A. B., what is the first care of every *Mason ?*' The correct answer to this would be : 'To study the useful rules in Architecture.' (See the first question and answer in the seventh section of the first Lecture.)

In the same Manual, in the 'Opening of the Lodge in the Second Degree,' the question stands thus : 'W. M.—Bro. J. W., what is the first care of every F. C. *Free*mason ?' Now, how shall we account for this discrepancy ? Surely if we are 'Freemasons' in the Second Degree, we are equally so in the First. There appears to be no way out of this dilemma.

The same inconsistency may be noticed in various places in several of the Rituals, and in Masonic publications, the words ' Masons' and ' Masonry ' occurring often in the same page, or even in the same paragraph, with 'Freemasons' and ' Freemasonry,'as though these opposing words were synonymous, and might be freely interchanged at will.

CHAPTER III.

The Lodge Room should be fitly arranged—The Form and Situation of the Lodge—The Position of the Door of Entrance—The Ornaments of the Lodge—The Furniture of the Lodge — The Jewels, Movable and Immovable — The Tracing Boards—The Rough and Perfect Ashlars—The Lewis—General Remarks.

IT may not be unprofitable for us to consider in some detail the Lodge room and its belongings : its Ornaments, Furniture, and Jewels. With regard to the Furniture, we shall discuss it, not only in the technical and restricted sense of the word, as it is described in the Explanation of the Tracing Board, and in the Lectures (that is, as consisting of the Volume of the Sacred Law, the Compasses, and the Square), but also in the more general acceptation of the term, including everything that is necessary for the decorous performance of the Ceremonies, and for the reasonable comfort and convenience of the Officers and the Brethren.

When 'the good man of the house' calls together 'his friends and his neighbours,' he makes all necessary arrangements for their reception, in order that they may derive the fullest enjoyment from his hospitality. This is the etiquette of private life. It should be with us also a matter of etiquette that our

Lodge room should be fitly arranged; that nothing be wanting, that all the means and appliances should be good of their kind, not mean or sordid, and, so far, unworthy of our Order; and especially that we should fulfil the conditions of the old adage, 'A place for everything, and everything in its place,' because without a proper arrangement of everything that may be used, or to which attention may be directed in the course of the several Ceremonies, the solemnity and the impressiveness of those Ceremonies may be considerably lessened, or altogether destroyed.

Unless the established order be strictly observed in the arrangement of the Lodge, and its Ornaments, Furniture, and Jewels, it (the Lodge) cannot be said to be properly prepared, or to be 'just, perfect and regular,' in the ordinary acceptation of the term; and the 'etiquette of Freemasonry' (in the sense of 'Forms which are observed in particular places') cannot be strictly maintained.

We will discuss these subjects consecutively, in the order in which they stand in the Explanation of the Tracing Board of the First Degree and in the First Lecture.

In the explanation of the Tracing Board of the First Degree the form of the Lodge is said to be 'an oblong square' (the correct term would be 'a rectangular oblong'), and its situation is described as being 'due east and west.' For the latter proposition full and sufficient reasons are given in the explanation of the Tracing Board.

It is highly desirable that these two conditions should be literally fulfilled whenever and wherever it may be possible. Too often, however, from circumstances which are beyond the control of the members of a Lodge, a literal fulfilment of the prescribed form and position is impossible.

Very many Lodges are compelled to hold their meetings in hotels or public rooms, the shape or the position (often both) of which do not agree with the model or ideal Lodge room. Frequently there is no alternative room in the locality, and nothing can be done but to make the best of existing circumstances, and to hold, in practice, that the Master's chair denotes the east, and the Senior Warden's the west, of the Lodge.

It is very desirable that the door of entrance should be in the west, or quasi-west, and, if possible, on the left of the Senior Warden's chair. In this position there are several advantages. 1. The position of the Junior Deacon being on the right of the Senior Warden, if the door be on his right hand also, the Junior Deacon and the Inner Guard will be thrown too nearly together; whereas if the door be on the left hand, then the Junior Deacon on the one side and the Inner Guard on the other, as it were, balance each other. The door being on the left of the Senior Warden, the Junior Warden and the Inner Guard are within clear view of each other, and members of the Lodge and visitors are, immediately on their entrance into the Lodge, brought under the direct notice of the Junior Warden. This is highly necessary, because he is responsible for all who enter, inasmuch as all announcements of the names of both members and visitors are made to him by the Inner

Guard. If the Candidate be admitted on the left of the Senior Warden, he is at once in the proper position for all that is to follow; from that starting-point he is enabled to make the complete perambulation of the Lodge, and on his return to the same place he is presented.

On the other hand, if he enter on the right he must pass the Senior Warden's chair twice—a course directly in contravention of the theory, that a Candidate for initiation must pass through three doorways —one real and two imaginary—before he is presented 'a candidate properly prepared,' etc. This theory of the three doorways will be fully elucidated in a future chapter.

Where, however, the door is on the right hand of the Senior Warden, and no change is possible, the tact of the Deacons and of the Director of Ceremonies must be exercised in order to minimize the awkwardness of the position.

The ornaments of the Lodge are the Mosaic Pavement, the Indented or Tessellated Border, and the Blazing Star or Glory in the centre. One sometimes sees in a Lodge a carpet of some conventional pattern upon the floor; this is highly objectionable, and forms a direct contradiction to the description given in the explanation of the Tracing Board previously quoted. It is happily becoming more and more rare in practice.

A carpet woven in the pattern of the Mosaic Pavement in black and white, or printed on felted drugget, is easily procurable—the latter at a small cost. A carpet the full size of the room, with a wide border, both of the prescribed pattern and colours, is highly desirable. In any case, 'the Blazing Star or Glory in the centre' should not be omitted.

'The furniture of the Lodge' consists of (comprises) 'the Volume of the Sacred Law, the Compasses, and the Square.' It is sad to find in some Lodges (probably few in number) that these indispensable furnishings of the Lodge are more or less mean and sordid in character—the Bible small, old, and dilapidated, and the Compasses and Square an ill-assorted couple : the Square of some common wood, the Compasses of brass, cheap and objectionable.

These things should not be. They show, first, a want of proper and becoming respect to the Volume of the Sacred Law, 'which is given to be the rule and guide of our faith and our actions ;' secondly, to the Compasses, the distinguishing Jewel of the Grand Master of our Order ; and thirdly, to the Square, the time-honoured emblem and cognizance of the Craft.

A handsomely-bound Bible of moderate size, and the Square and Compasses *in silver*, will scarcely be beyond the means of any Lodge. They are often presented by zealous and liberal Brethren to their respective Lodges, and in such cases the gifts are almost invariably worthy of the givers and of the recipients.

The Jewels comprise 'three movable and three immovable.' 'The movable jewels are the Square, the Level, and the Plumb-rule.' 'They are called movable jewels because they are worn by the Master, and the Senior and Junior Wardens during the period of their tenure of their several offices, and are transferred to their successors on the day of installation.' The collars bearing these several jewels should be placed upon the pedestals, respectively, of the Master and the Wardens, previously to the opening of the Lodge.

'The immovable jewels are the Tracing Board, and the Rough and the Perfect Ashlar.' 'They are called immovable jewels because they lie open and unmoved, each in its appointed place in the Lodge, for the Brethren to moralize upon.'

With regard to the position of the Tracing Boards, there is much difference in practice in different Lodges. In some old Lodges they are simply the canvases not framed, and they are laid upon the floor (each according to the Degree in which the Lodge is opened). This plan is objectionable chiefly in consequence of the damage and defacement likely to ensue.

In other Lodges the three Tracing Boards are framed and are hung upon the walls of the Lodge room. By this arrangement they are better secured from damage; but it not unfrequently happens that the whole of the three are left upon the walls, irrespectively of the Ceremony which is being performed. Clearly, during an initiation the Tracing Boards of the Second and Third Degrees should not be exposed to view, and during the Ceremony of Passing the Tracing Board of the Third Degree should be kept concealed.

As regards Biblical, and even traditional, accuracy, the present Tracing Boards leave much to be desired, especially the second and the third. Some of our artist Brethren could design a set which would be artistic, and at the same time correctly in accordance with each of the three Degrees.

For some further remarks upon the Tracing Boards of the three Degrees, see Appendix B, page 236.

The proper place for the Rough Ashlar is on the floor in front of the Junior Warden's pedestal (not *on* the pedestal, as one sometimes sees it placed) ; it is there in full view. The stone should not be quite 'rough and unhewn, as when taken from the quarry.' This is intended 'for the Entered Apprentice to work, mark, and indent upon.' It should show evidence of having been so worked, marked, and indented ; it should be as though a succession of E. A.'s had tried their ''prentice hand' upon it ; had indeed *rough-hewn* it with the Gavel, and had knocked off some at least of the 'superfluous knobs and ex-crescences.'

Indications might also be shown of some rudi-mentary work with the Chisel, this working tool being presented to the Entered Apprentice in order that he may with it 'further smooth and prepare the stone for the hands of the more expert Craftsman.'

The Perfect Ashlar is 'a stone of a true die ; a perfect cube.' The severest test to which the skill of an operative Mason can be submitted is the pro-duction of a perfect cube. It has even been asserted that a *perfect* cube has never yet been produced. Its position should be immediately in front of the Senior Warden's pedestal, *properly suspended, with the Lewis inserted in the centre.*

A few words may with advantage be here added upon the manner in which the Perfect Ashlar is or may be suspended in the Lodge. The explanation of the Lewis, as it is given in the 'Explanation of the

First Tracing Board,' runs thus : 'It is formed of three pieces of metal, the two outermost of which are dovetailed in shape ; these are attached to the end of a chain by a movable pin. The implement thus formed, when properly inserted in a mortice made to receive it, enables the Operative Mason to raise the stone to the necessary elevation, and to lower it into its appointed position without any ligature whatever.'

This may be seen in operation during the erection of any edifice which is being built wholly or partially of stone, and notably in the case of the laying of a foundation or chief corner-stone, at which some Masonic or other ceremony of a public character is observed.

It will readily be seen that a chain or rope passed *round* the stone, and especially the keystone of an arch, would prevent its being properly bedded in its place. Nothing could answer the purpose more effectually than the Lewis, which, with slight—if, indeed, any—modification in its form, has been for many centuries an indispensable implement in Operative Masonry ; while in Speculative Masonry it has from time immemorial been one of the most interesting and expressive of the Symbols of our Order.

In some old Lodges one may sometimes see a curious and complicated structure, consisting of a crane with a windlass, on a platform (a cumbrous affair, generally broken or otherwise out of order), for the purpose of suspending the Perfect Ashlar. It may be interesting from its age, but it takes up too much room, and is altogether inconvenient wherever it may be placed in the Lodge.

A very simple plan of construction is to have three quasi scaffold poles, about three feet or a little over in length, with their bases fixed to a flat triangle, and with a 'tackle and fall,' and a 'cleet' to which the end of the cord is made fast; the poles are tapered, and, of course, are brought together at the top. This plan is neat, inexpensive, and efficient, and at the same time it has the merit of being a model, in miniature, of that which is in constant use in Operative Masonry in laying foundation-stones, etc.

CHAPTER IV.

THE WORKING TOOLS, COLUMNS, ETC.

The Gavel—The 'Walling Hammer' of Operative Masonry—
The Columns and the Orders of Architecture—Discussion re-
garding the Ionic and Doric Orders—Some Ancient Land-
marks—Freemasonry is a Progressive Science—The Pedestals
—The Chairs—The Furniture of some Old Lodges—The
Daïs—Those who should occupy the Daïs—Platform for the
Master's Chair—Reception of Visiting Brethren—The
Wardens' Chairs—On the manner in which the Principal
Officers should take and leave their Chairs—Manner of in-
ducting a *locum tenens*—Following the true course of the Sun.

THE second in order of the Working Tools of the
Entered Apprentice Degree is the Gavel. This is
presented to the Worshipful Master when he is installed into the Chair, as the Gavel is the emblem of
authority; yet one sees occasionally in the Lodge, the
Master, and the Wardens, each with—not a Gavel—
but a light Mall (a miniature copy of the heavy Mall
of the Third Degree), that is a small mallet with a
turned head, whereas the Gavel has a slightly elongated
head, with one end *flat-faced* like a hammer, the
other end having a blunt axe edge.

This shape is admirably adapted to the work which
it is represented as being designed to perform, namely,
'to knock off all superfluous knobs and excrescences.'
An actual working tool of the operative mason of the
present day is really a Gavel, with the head longer

than that which we use; it is called a 'Walling Hammer.'

It is highly desirable that the regulation Gaveis should be used in every Lodge. They are supplied in sets of three, bearing respectively the emblem of the Master, and of the Senior and the Junior Warden. They can be procured at a small cost from those who supply lodge furniture. (No mention need be made of the 24-inch Gauge and the Chisel.)

The Working Tools of the Second and Third Degrees are, with rare exceptions, generally appropriate, and in order. In newly-formed Lodges it may be said that they are invariably so, having been generally purchased in the sets complete; but in some old Lodges we find notable exceptions, such as a nonde script Level or Compasses, and far too often a common *lead-pencil* instead of the port-crayon.

The Columns of the Senior and the Junior Warden frequently bear little or no indication of the Order in Architecture which they are severally said to represent. In the address to the Senior Warden, after he has been placed in the chair in the west, his column is described as representing the Doric Order, and that of the Junior Warden as being of the Corinthian Order; and in each case it is highly desirable that they should be fair representations of those orders.

Some discussion (probably confined to two or three provinces) took place a few years ago as to the three Orders in Architecture represented by the several Columns of the Worshipful Master and the two Wardens, and as to the quality assigned to each. The older Rituals give the Doric Column to the

Master, and assign to it the quality of Wisdom ; the Ionic Column they give to the Senior Warden, and assign to it the quality of Strength ; and the Corinthian, with its quality of Beauty, to the Junior Warden. About the last there has been no difference of opinion, but the appropriateness of the qualities assigned respectively to the other two cannot be maintained with any show of reason.

The opponents of the older definition justly argued that the Doric Column, in its sturdy proportions and its spare ornamentation, represents the quality of Strength in a far greater degree than the more slender and more ornate Ionic Column can be said to do. The upholders of the older form replied, in effect, that from time immemorial, both in the Explanation of the Tracing Board of the First Degree, and in the Lecture, priority of place has always been given to the Doric Column, associated with the quality of Wisdom, and that this Doric Column has always been assigned to the Worshipful Master.

The difference of opinion and of practice thus set forth still exists to a considerable extent. In the older Lodges, and indeed, with rare exceptions throughout many provinces, the old order of sequence remains unchanged ; it is clung to as tenaciously as though it were a veritable landmark of our Order, in the same way as the author of these pages has heard it maintained that the old form of the answer to one of the questions—previously to the passing—namely, ' The sun being a *fixed body*, and the earth, etc.,' is a landmark, and must not be removed. Similarly, he has quite recently heard the assertion that to another of the same set of questions, the old form of answer, 'free by birth,' constitutes a landmark, the resolution duly passed by Grand Lodge to the contrary notwithstanding; and in direct contradiction to the words 'a free man,' in Clause 187 of the Book of Constitutions.

Of a truth these *Landmarks* (falsely so-called) are great stumbling-blocks in the way of 'progressive improvement.' Brethren who endeavour to eliminate from our Ceremonies the misstatements, the anachronisms, and the solecisms, which in the course of time have crept into our working; or to correct misquotations, or errors of grammar, are constantly met by the alarum-cry, 'The Landmarks are in danger,' in any rectification of error which they may advocate. Yet the very men who raise this cry will, in performing the Ceremony of the Second Degree, gravely assure the candidate that 'Freemasonry is a *progressive* science.'

It is right to mention that the Columns now supplied by those who sell Lodge furniture are made to correspond with the newer idea of the several Orders in Architecture, and the respective qualities ascribed to each; thus the Ionic, representing Wisdom, is assigned to the Worshipful Master; the Doric, representing Strength, to the Senior Warden; and the Corinthian, representing Beauty, to the Junior Warden. Nevertheless, as before observed, the older order remains unchanged in many of the older Lodges.

The memory of the writer recurs to the strongly expressed opinions of the Provincial Grand Secretary of a Northern Province, and to a letter from an eminent Scottish Freemason, both being upon this subject. They both condemned the newer view of the question as an 'innovation upon the body of Freemasonry;' in effect, they took a similar view upon this question to that which was held by a certain potentate with regard to grammar. He said that 'his imperial rank set him far above the rules of grammar.' So these men contended (in effect) that the ancient dicta of Freemasonry were to be held to be above the rules and Orders of Architecture !

The pedestals of the Worshipful Master, and of the Senior and Junior Warden, should be graduated in size, in accordance with the difference in rank of these Officers. Each should bear on the front the Working Tool by which each Officer is specially distinguished, namely, the Square for the Master, the Level for the Senior Warden, and the Plumb-rule for the Junior Warden. These may be really working tools, of the size and make of those in use in the Second Degree, securely fixed in the centre of the front of the pedestal. The effect of this is bolder and better than when the emblem is painted or gilt on the pedestal.

The three chairs should be large and grandiose in character. In one Lodge known to the writer, the chairs are made each in strict accordance with the Order in Architecture assigned to each of the three principal Officers. They are spacious, well proportioned, and very handsome. The pedestals also correspond to the three Orders: that is, they have each two columns; the bases, the shafts, and the capitals of each pair of columns being perfectly true to each of the three Orders. That which we may call the box part of the pedestal is recessed in the two front corners, so as to leave room for the columns. The top of each pedestal and the plinth are in the usual form, a rectangular oblong. The candlesticks also represent severally the columns of the Ionic, the Doric, and the Corinthian Orders. These are nearly, or quite the height of the three pedestals, beside which they stand in the Lodge.

This set of furniture is remarkable for the contrast which it forms to the furniture of some of the old Lodges in country districts—awful examples of barbaric taste (the production, probably, of the eighteenth century)—in which the fancy of the maker has run riot, in curious shapes, and scrolls, and foliage, wonderful to behold, and as far as the poles are asunder removed from any known Order in Architecture.

Comparatively few Lodges are, at the present day, without a daïs, or raised platform, at the eastern end of the Lodge. No Lodge-room can be considered to be complete without it. Upon this daïs the Worshipful Master and Past Masters alone are expected to sit. An exception may be—perhaps should be—made in favour of the Chaplain, who, by virtue of his office, should be considered to be entitled to a seat somewhat raised above the level of the ordinary members of the Lodge. His place should be at the extreme end of the daïs. An additional platform is almost invariably provided for the Master's chair, so that he may be raised above the level of the Past Masters. This platform should be from seven to eight inches high, the daïs itself being of about the same elevation. It is very desirable that all the chairs (if chairs be used) upon the Daïs should be of fair commodious proportions. In Lodges where the room is kept exclusively for Masonic uses handsome, well-padded, continuous seats are generally provided on the daïs if they be not continued round the room.

Every visiting brother, who is either the Master of a Lodge or a Past Master, should, immediately upon his entrance into the Lodge, be conducted by the Director of Ceremonies (or, in his absence, should be invited by the Worshipful Master) to a seat on the daïs. If all the seats there are occupied it will be in accordance with etiquette—and, indeed, with ordinary politeness—that a member of the Lodge shall give place in favour of the visiting brother.

Each of the Wardens' chairs should stand upon a platform (seven to eight inches high). All the three pedestals should stand upon the floor ; consequently they should be of sufficient height to allow for the elevation of the platform, and in the case of the Master's pedestal for the platform and the daïs combined. It is by no means uncommon *in outlying districts* to see tall pedestals and the Wardens' chairs standing on the floor (that is, without a platform), the result being that those officers partially disappear when they sit down.

In taking their places in their respective chairs, the Worshipful Master and the Wardens should invariably follow the course of the Sun ; that is, the Master should enter on the North side and leave on the South. The Senior Warden should enter on the

South, and leave on the North side ; and the Junior Warden should enter on the East side, and leave on the West. During the ceremonies, when the Master leaves his place in order to communicate the S..., etc., and the Senior Warden leaves his chair in order to invest the Candidate, they should, on resuming their several positions, pass round and re-enter their respective places on the side opposite to that by which they left them.

When from any cause either of the Principal Officers leaves his chair for any appreciable period of time another Brother should take his place. In such cases a good custom prevails—in probably the majority of Lodges—namely, the Officer who is leaving his chair takes the right hand of the Brother who is to take his place, and, as it were, inducts him into the chair which he himself has vacated. If, and when, the proper Officer returns, his *locum tenens* offers his right hand, and assists the officer back into his chair in the same manner, this is true politeness, and therefore true etiquette ; it has in it a grace and dignity worthy of our Ancient and Illustrious Order.

The reason why the Principal Officers should always enter and leave their several chairs in the manner thus described is the same as that which prescribes that the Candidates in each degree should be led ' up the North, past the Worshipful Master in the East, down the South, and be conducted to the Senior Warden in the West,' namely, that we follow 'the true course of the Sun, which rises in the East, gains its meridian lustre in the South, and sets in the West.' (*Vide* Lecture in the First Degree.)

CHAPTER V.

THE PERFECT EQUIPMENT OF A LODGE.

Manner of Brethren moving about in the Lodge—Selection of
Password for leaving the Lodge—Charter or Warrant to be
hung in a Convenient Place—Alms-dish, Kneeling-stool, and
Kneeling-cushion—Constitutions and By laws should be given
to every Brother—Convenience of Provincial Calendars—
Interchange of Visits—Every Lodge should have an Organ or
Harmonium—Musical Services on the Increase—Office and
Duties of Organist—Contrast between a Ceremony with and
without Music—Coffin and ' White Gloves ' should be Abo-
lished — Defence of Elaboration of Detail in this Book —
Everything should be done ' Decently and in Order '—No
desire to promulgate Fads or Crotchets, nor ' to make innovation in the body of Freemasonry.'

In the previous chapter an explanation was given of
the custom in our Lodges of the perambulations
being always made in one direction, namely, that
which follows the true course of the Sun. Upon this
principle it is very desirable—indeed, it is a constant
custom in many Lodges—that a Brother who is
seated on the North side of the Lodge, if he wishes
to go to the South or the West, should not go thither
directly, but should go to the East, and pass in front
of the Master's pedestal, and salute in passing, according to the Degree in which the Lodge may be at
the time. If he have to pass the Junior Warden he
should salute him in the same manner, and the same
if he passes the Senior Warden.

Another useful custom prevails in many Lodges,

and is worthy of general adoption ; it is this : The Worshipful Master selects a password for each meeting ; this he communicates to the Junior Warden and to the Inner Guard. When any Brother wishes to leave the Lodge he obtains this password from either the Master or the Junior Warden ; he then gives the word to the Inner Guard, thus in effect showing that he has permission to leave the Lodge. This is in strict accordance with the instruction contained in the address by the Investing Master (or Officer) to the Inner Guard, which runs thus : 'It will be your duty at all times to obey the commands of the Junior Warden, and to see that no one either enters or *leaves* the Lodge without his permission, or that of the Worshipful Master.'

In the great majority of Lodges the Charter, or Warrant, is framed and hung in a convenient place, not too far from the East end of the Lodge. This important document is thus preserved from soil or other injury, and being well in view, the Worshipful Master can point to it when he informs the Candidate that 'under it the Lodge is authorized to hold its meetings,' etc.

Mention was made in an earlier chapter of an Alms-dish. It is very desirable that something should be provided specially for this purpose. A decent silver-plated or brass salver can be procured for a few shillings. A kneeling-stool in front of the Master's pedestal is now almost universally provided ; thus superseding the necessity of using a chair for the Candidate during the Ob.... A kneeling-cushion is also desirable for use in the West.

In many Lodges, during the concluding portion of the Ceremony of Initiation, a copy of the Book of Constitutions, together with one of the By-laws of the Lodge, is *really presented* to every newly Initiated Brother, to remain in his own possession.* This is an excellent custom. The newly-admitted Brother naturally is desirous to gain all the knowledge that is possible to him of the nature and the Constitution of the Fraternity of which he has become a member. When the copies are merely shown to the Novice, and retained by the Worshipful Master, it is improbable that the new member will take the trouble (involving also trouble to others) to go to the Lodge for the ' serious perusal ' of those books ; whereas, if they be really given, he takes them to his home, and at his ease he can read them with the attention and carefulness which have been recommended to him by the Worshipful Master, and which the zeal born of his recent Initiation will lead him to follow literally, and with profit to himself in the way of ' Masonic knowledge,' in which in the Charge he is told that he is to make ' daily progress.' The desirability of every member of the Craft possessing a copy of the Book of Constitutions led to its being produced at the present low price (one shilling and sixpence), and the Constitutions require (as shown) that every member of a Lodge should have a copy of its own By-laws.

Calendars are now published in many Provinces, containing the day, the hour, and the place of meeting of every Lodge within the Province ; and many

* Section 163 of the Book of Constitutions enjoins that a copy of the By-laws should be so presented to every member.

Lodges year by year send a copy to every subscribing member. The convenience of possessing such a Calendar is very great in many ways. A Brother is enabled on reference to his Calendar to make his engagements, so that he may be free to attend his own Lodge, or to visit any other to which inclination or duty may lead him. The word duty is used advisedly, because it is highly desirable that a kind and fraternal feeling should exist between neighbouring Lodges; and nothing tends so much to create and to foster this feeling as the interchange of visits between the several members of the Lodges in a district. The Principal Officers, especially, should consider it a part of their duty (see Section 149, B. of C.) to set a good example in this respect. Something may be, and often is, gained in Masonic Knowledge by the interchange of such visits.

An organ or harmonium is happily now considered to be an indispensable item in the furnishing of a Lodge. The adoption of musical services, both vocal and instrumental, is on the increase; hence the office of Organist has become much less of a sinecure than it used to be. His duties are set forth in the address delivered to him when he is invested with the jewel of his Office, as follows:

ORGANIST.

Bro. ......, I have great pleasure in investing you as Organist. Your Jewel, the Lyre, is the emblem of Music, one of the seven liberal Arts and Sciences, the study of which is inculcated in the Fellow-Crafts' Degree. The records of Ancient History, both sacred

and secular, testify that from the earliest times Music
has borne a more or less important part in the celebra-
tion of religious rites and ceremonies; that Pagans
and Monotheists, the Ancient Hebrews, and the
more comparatively modern Christians, have in all
ages made full and free use of music, as an aid to
devotion, and in the expression of praise and thanks-
giving in the services of their several systems of
religion. In like manner, Freemasonry, from the
earliest period of its history, has availed itself of the
aid of music in the performance of its rites and
ceremonies; and we must all feel how much of
impressiveness and solemnity is derived from the
judicious introduction of vocal and instrumental music
into those ceremonies. Music has been defined as
'the concord of sweet sounds.' In this aspect it
typifies the concord and harmony which have always
been among the foremost characteristics of our Order.
Your Jewel, therefore, the emblem of Concord, should
stimulate us to promote and to maintain concord,
goodwill, and affection, not only among the members
of our own Lodge, but with all Brethren of the Craft.
(This address is taken from the Revised Ritual,
page 317.)

Little further need be added upon the subject of
the musical services in the three degrees; any Brother
who visits other Lodges occasionally, or frequently, is
able to mark the contrast between a Ceremony
performed with accompanying vocal and instrumental
music, and one without that accompaniment, and in
which the voice of the Worshipful Master alone is·
heard from the beginning to the end, with only the

slight break here and there of the little which the Wardens have to say. The impression made upon the mind of the Candidate by the musical addition to the Ceremony is far deeper, and consequently is calculated to be far more enduring, than that formed by a Ceremony unrelieved by the effect of the Divine Art of Music. (See Appendix M, page 271.)

Among the requisites indispensable in the furnishing of a Lodge are the 'Emblems of Mortality.' It is much to be regretted that the Coffin, sometimes in miniature, sometimes full size, or a flat board like the lid of a Coffin, should so often be found in our Lodges. The Coffin was utterly unknown in the East in the time of King Solomon; the use of the bier and the winding sheet was universal. A number of instances of the latter form of burial may be found in the Old and in the New Testament. (For specific cases see Appendix C, page 240.)

It is equally to be regretted that the allusion to the Coffin retains its place in quite recently published Rituals; as does also the mention of the fifteen trusty Fellow-Crafts, attending the obsequies of H. A. B., in *white gloves !* and the hint of the probability that the body would have been buried in the Holy of Holies but for a prohibition to the contrary; which prohibition is not to be found in the Bible, the words used being taken from the New Testament, where they are applied to quite a different subject. (See Appendix D, page 240.)

Some, probably many, of the subjects discussed, with more or less of elaboration of detail, in this and the previous Chapters, may be considered to be either unnecessary, because they treat of things in constant use in every Lodge ; or that more has been said than there is a positive necessity to say. The thought will naturally arise in the minds of some readers of these pages : 'All these requisites for a Lodge, and the mode of arrangement, etc., are to be found continually in the Lodge of which I am a member, and in the majority of those which I occasionally visit ; then why this long repetition of detail, of things with which we are perfectly familiar ?' This may be true, but such a Brother must know that there are many hundreds of Lodges, lying beyond the sphere of his observation, and which, from various causes, are very far indeed from coming up to the standard of perfect equipment such as the proper performance of our Rites and Ceremonies demands.

Those among us who have had a lengthened experience in Freemasonry, and who have been frequent visitors in many lodges, in different—and in some cases, widely separated—Provinces, know that there is too often a want of carefulness in details, and in arrangement, and a deficiency in certain necessary things, which ought not to be the case in any Lodge of Freemasons. A state of incompleteness incompatible with the duty of a Director of Ceremonies, and indeed of every Officer of the Lodge, namely, that he shall see ' that everything be done decently and in order.'

To sum up briefly, it may be said with entire truthfulness that a want of acquaintance with, or a great degree of disregard of, the 'Etiquette of Freemasonry ' exists in too many of our Lodges ; and that both in 'the forms which are observed in particular places,' and in the other portion of the meaning of the word etiquette, namely, 'regulations as to behaviour, dress, etc., to be observed by particular persons upon particular occasions,' many of our Lodges and their members are more or less open to improvement.

It is with the view and in the hope of effecting changes where they may be proved to be necessary that these pages have been written : not in any censorious or captious spirit, nor with any desire to promulgate fads or crotchets, nor, above all, 'to make innovation in the body of Freemasonry;' but, in perfect singleness of mind and heart, to give the results in plain language of the experience gained during an unusually protracted and varied Masonic career, in the hope and trust that some instruction may be imparted, and possibly some improvements may be effected where the need of improvement may be felt to exist. So mote it be.

CHAPTER VI.

DRESS, JEWELS, AND PUNCTUAL ATTENDANCE.

Evening Dress is the Rule, but not Universal—Difficulties in
the way of Evening Dress—Some Lodges put it in the Circular
—Uniformity in Dress desirable—Anecdote of a Brother in
Tweed—A Contrast : Installation of the late Duke of Albany
as W. M. of the Apollo Lodge, Oxford—Jewels which may be
worn in a Craft Lodge or a Royal Arch Chapter—Miniature
Jewels—Memorials of Gratitude—Grand or Provincial Grand
Clothing—Undress Clothing—The Black Tie not in order—
Advice of Polonius applicable—Punctuality in Attendance—
The Time stated should be the Time—The Evils of Unpunc-
tuality—An Illustrative Anecdote—Knife and Fork Masons.

In discussing 'the Etiquette of Freemasonry,' the question of dress naturally suggests itself for consideration.
We may briefly state the conclusions at which the
consensus of opinion and of practice, in the great
majority of cases, would appear to have arrived. In
Lodges where the members dine together after the
business of the Lodge is concluded, evening dress is
the rule. This is, indeed, so general that it may
almost be said to be invariable and universal.

In other Lodges, where a supper or some moderate
refreshment is provided, evening dress is not universal.
Still, in some even of these the Brethren make it a
rule to wear full evening dress both at their own
meetings and when visiting other Lodges. The difficulty in the way of this graceful custom is, that the

interval between the cessation of the professional or business avocations of many of the members, and the hour for the meeting of the Lodge, will not allow time sufficient for an entire change of dress.

In cities and large towns, where, in the Lodges, the Initiations are more or less frequent, there are often two, and occasionally three Ceremonies to be performed on the same evening, and necessarily the hour for meeting must be comparatively early. This will probably account for the fact that many members have acquired the habit of attending the Lodge in the habiliments of ordinary every-day life. In this respect each Lodge is, as a rule, governed by its own custom. and usage ; but the members should strive, where it is necessary, rather to attain to a higher standard of propriety in the matter of dress than to degenerate to a lower level.

In certain Lodges the circular states thus : ' Dress, full black, white tie and gloves.' This at least may be expected of every member, whatever be his circumstances in life, and every effort should be made by those in authority in the Lodge to promote uniformity in this respect, as far as may be done, without wounding the susceptibilities of any individual member who from any cause may deviate from the general rule. When, however, as unfortunately sometimes happens, a member comes into the Lodge in a noticeable mixed costume, or something in strong contrast to the general tone of the dress of the members, one feels inclined to apply a rebuke to him, such as that addressed to the guest in the Parable, who came to the marriage-feast ' not having on a wedding garment.'

An instance of this breach of etiquette recurs to the writer's memory. He was at the time Master of a Lodge in one of our great seats of learning, and attended a meeting of the Provincial Grand Lodge to receive the Jewel of an Office to which he had been appointed. At this meeting a comparatively young man—an undergraduate—who had also been appointed to Office, presented himself for investiture clad in a light-coloured, shaggy suit of tweed, or something of that kind—a new fashion at that time. The Provincial Grand Master hesitated as to whether or not he would cancel the appointment, but ignorance of the custom as to costume was pleaded, the brother having never before attended such a meeting, and a very humble apology was tendered. The Provincial Grand Master relented ; but he administered a rebuke, as severe as words could make it, upon such a flagrant violation of Masonic Etiquette. That undergraduate went away ' a sadder, but a wiser man.'

Another memory in direct contrast to the foregoing instance may be here given. The writer was present when the late lamented Duke of Albany—then Prince Leopold—was installed as Worshipful Master of the Apollo (University) Lodge in Oxford. Upon that occasion the Prince, together with the retiring Master, certain of the Past Masters, and *every Officer of the Lodge*, wore knee-tights and silver-buckled shoes, and, in addition, the Prince wore the ' Garter.' No suit of ' dittoes,' nor any other incongruity of dress was to be seen on that day ; or on the next day, when the Prince was installed as Provincial Grand Master of Oxfordshire. The meeting for the latter Ceremony was held in the Sheldonian Theatre.

While we are discussing that branch of our subject which relates to ' dress,' a few words may be said about the Jewels which may or may not be worn in the Lodge. Few of our members are ignorant of the rule which strictly forbids the wearing in a Craft Lodge of a Jewel belonging to any Degree which is not recognised by, and is not under the authority of, the Grand Lodge. To this rule there is positively no exception, and yet occasionally, not often, one sees a brother enter the Lodge wearing the Jewel of the Mark, or some other by-degree, and even that of the Knights-Templar.

It is true that H.R.H. the Grand Master is a member. and has past rank in both of these Degrees, but although he is at the head of one of them, Grand Lodge does not recognise them, nor exercise jurisdiction over them in any way ; therefore the Jewels of those Degrees are not allowed to be worn in a Craft Lodge. The case of the Royal Arch Degree is entirely different from these ; H.R.H. the Duke of Connaught is Grand Superintendent of the Order, and the Grand Secretary in the Craft is always Grand Scribe E. in the Grand Chapter of Royal Arch Masons, consequently all the Jewels of the Royal Arch Degree may be worn in a Craft Lodge.

The Jewels which may with perfect propriety be worn in a Craft Lodge (and a Royal Arch Chapter also) are the Master Mason's, Past Master's, Past Steward of either or all of the Charities, and the Jewel commemorating the Jubilee of Her late Majesty, the late Patroness of our Order ; also the Jewels of the Royal Arch Degree, whether of ordinary Royal Arch Masons,

or of Present or Past First Principals, or Present or
Past Grand, or Provincial, or District Grand Principals, and some others which need not be specified,
with this special reservation, that they must belong
to either the Craft or the Royal Arch Degree, and no
other. Miniature Jewels, each being a facsimile in
design of the full size Jewels, are now very frequently
worn by Brethren who, from having served as
Stewards of the Charities and otherwise, have become
entitled to wear a considerable number of these
honourable badges of distinction.

Many of these Jewels have been presented to the
wearers, and are the memorials of the gratitude of
their several Lodges for eminent, and often long-con-
tinued services, and which the recipients may well
feel pleasure and pride in wearing. They are something more than mere personal adornments; they
subserve an excellent purpose, by inciting younger
brethren to increased zeal and energy in the work of
the Lodge. 'The hope of reward sweetens labour,'
and when work is sweetened by hope and lightened
by zeal, it becomes a labour of love; and 'profit' to
the Lodge, and 'pleasure' to the worker, 'will be the
result.'

With regard to the wearing of Grand, or Provincial
Grand clothing, much difference of opinion and of
practice exists. Many—probably the majority of—
brethren have undress aprons and collars, which they
always wear at the ordinary meetings of their own
Lodge; some even of these wear full dress if visiting
a Lodge other than their own, even if it be a regular
meeting of the Lodge which they are visiting. Upon

Festivals, or other occasions out of the ordinary way, they would, as a matter of course, wear full-dress clothing, with all proper insignia appertaining thereto, either in their own or in any other Lodge. Instances are not wanting of brethren considering it to be their duty to wear the full-dress clothing upon every occasion during the year of their tenure of Grand or Provincial Grand Office. No reason can be urged against their doing so. There is no hard and fast rule upon the subject. Customs vary in different districts, and individual taste seems to be the chief guide in this matter.

At all the regular meetings of Grand Lodge, and of Provincial, and of District Lodges, full dress clothing is invariably worn. At meetings of Provincial, or of District Lodges, upon special occasions other than the regular meetings, Provincial or District Grand Masters often allow undress clothing to be worn. On all occasions when the full-dress clothing is worn, the traditional white tie and gloves should be worn—a comparatively recent fashion of wearing black ties for full dress, to the contrary, notwithstanding. The black tie is not 'in accordance with the ancient usage and established custom of the Order' in this respect.

In short, we should show—in so far as outward observance can show—our estimation of, and our respect for, Freemasonry, by always being fitly attired in the Lodge. The advice of Polonius to his son Laertes is of very wide application; it suits the case in question :

> ' Costly thy habit as thy purse can buy,
> But not expressed in fancy ; rich, not gaudy ;
> For the apparel oft proclaims the man.'

Very little needs to be said upon the subject of punctuality in attendance on the part of both Officers and brethren; but it can hardly be passed over without notice. In these days of railway locomotion, and of high pressure generally in business matters, sharp time is as a rule obliged to be observed by all sorts and conditions of men in the affairs of the outer world. The same rule should, by every possible means, be applied to the meetings of the Lodge. One well-known case may here be cited. The newly-installed Master announced his full determination to open the Lodge upon every occasion punctually at the hour stated in the summons. He was well supported in this decision by his Officers; he and they were always clothed and in their seats *before the time*, and as the hour struck, the Master's gavel sounded the note of preparation, and certainly during that year the general attendance was far more punctual and not less numerous than it had been theretofore.

The time stated upon the summons should be understood to mean that time, and not half an hour or an hour later, and all who attend the Lodge, more especially the Officers, should so regard it. In the address to the Wardens after their investiture, and their induction into their respective chairs, the following sentence occurs, 'You are expected to be patterns of good order, of *regularity in attendance*, etc.' Regularity in this sense cannot be separated from punctuality, and the precept applies with equal force to all the Officers of the Lodge. Their acceptance of their several Offices should be taken virtually as a pledge that, with the honour, they also acknowledge their responsibility for a faithful and *punctual* performance of their several duties to the best of their skill and ability.

Unpunctuality, to which is due the frequent paucity in numbers when the Lodge is opened, and even during a Ceremony which may be performed at the earlier portion of the meeting, is not only a bad compliment and a great discouragement to the Worshipful Master : it also produces a bad impression in the mind of new members, and especially those upon whom the Ceremony is being performed.

A personal reminiscence will show the inconvenience and annoyance resulting from the habit of unpunctuality on the part of members of a Lodge. The writer was invited to attend an Anniversary Festival, and to perform the Ceremony of Installation in a rural district (about two hours' journey from his home), situated on a branch railway, single line of rails, trains few and far between. He reached the place *before* the time appointed. Half an hour *after* the appointed time two or three members lounged in and began to assist the Tyler in preparing the Lodge. *A full hour after time* the Lodge was opened ; some routine business was transacted, the balance-sheet was presented, etc., all in a leisurely manner, with the result that the Installation was barely completed in time for the last train home. Not one minute to spare for necessary refreshment ; the olfactories regaled with the appetising odours of the dinner then waiting to be served. Finale, home reached after an unbroken fast of nine hours—since lunch at 1.30. This serves to point a moral appropriate to the subject under consideration.

One used to hear, *years ago*, of members who were seldom in the Lodge, 'when the Brethren were at labour,' and seldom absent 'when they were at refreshment,' thereby gaining for themselves the title of 'knife and fork Freemasons.' This, however, belongs to an age now happily passed away, and with it the reputation for an inordinate love of feasting, which to some extent our Order once had, as many now living can well remember.

CHAPTER VII.

THE TYLER AND HIS MULTIFARIOUS DUTIES.

What manner of man the Tyler should be—Three Classes of Tyler—A Custom with certain Advantages—Serving Brethren —Retired Non-Commissioned Officers make Good Tylers— A rare and noteworthy Experience—The Duties of the Tyler —Unqualified Intruders—Admission of Visitors—Assistance of the Junior Warden—The Preparation of Candidates—The Tyler responsible for all the belongings of the Lodge and for its preparation—The Tyler's Duties closely connected with the subject of this book.

IT will be convenient at this stage of our work to consider in some detail the multifarious duties of that very useful Officer the Tyler, some of whose duties will be found to have a distinct bearing upon our subject. We will first, however, discuss briefly the Tyler himself, and consider what manner of man he should be. Experience gained in a number of different Lodges enables one to divide them into at least three classes. The first of these would consist of old Past Masters ; these are now comparatively few in number, and are gradually becoming more and more rarely to be found.

These may be sub-divided into two classes, one class consisting of those who continue to subscribe to the Lodge and are unwilling to be out of Office, and who perform the duties of Tyler with perfect

5

efficiency without fee or reward.*   The other sub-division will include those 'who perhaps from circumstances of unforeseen calamity,' etc., are glad to retain their connection with Freemasonry by serving the Office of Tyler, the fees of membership being remitted, and the small emoluments of the Office being of value to them in their low estate.

The second main division would comprise members of certain Lodges in which it is the custom to have no permanent Tyler, paid or otherwise, that Office being year by year filled by a junior member, and constituting the first step upon the Official ladder, and without which no one can attain to any higher Office.

This custom has certain advantages ; it goes to the very root of the matter, and if the aspirant should go on step by step through all the gradations of Office, until he attains to the chair of Worshipful Master, his experience will be unquestionable, and he will have the satisfaction of feeling that, having begun at the very beginning, he had literally worked his way upward to the Chair.   Against this custom may be set the disadvantages of the want of age and of experience in the work of the Lodge.   Zeal and ability, care and attention, will, however, soon enable even the youngest in experience to perform his duty with a fair degree of efficiency and success.

The third, and by far the most numerous division, will comprise those who are paid for their services (excluding the second sub-division of the Past Masters mentioned in the first division).   Some of

* See page 68, for a case of one of this sort.

these are Initiated with this express intention ; they are called 'serving brethren,' and in many Lodges they act as waiters at Banquets, etc. Where Lodges are held in Hotels, it is not unfrequently thought desirable to initiate one of the waiters (preferably the head of his department), but in this case he does not always undertake the duties of Tyler.

Other paid Tylers are older Freemasons (who have not passed the Chair) who have fallen upon evil days, and who are glad to serve the Lodge in a humble capacity, and to receive the small emoluments of the Office, and who rank as ordinary members of the Lodge, but without paying any subscriptions. These are as a rule faithful and efficient Officers, zealous and energetic in the performance of their duties.

Some mention should be made of those who have formerly been members of Military Lodges—generally pensioners—and, foremost among these, retired non-commissioned officers are especially to be commended. If they possess medals and a goodly number of clasps, and have testimonials of good conduct, as most of them have, so much the better. Old soldiers, if they have encouraged habits of sobriety, may be depended upon to keep sober under all circumstances. They have in addition learned the lesson of perfect obedience ; they have been accustomed to rigid discipline, and have become strict disciplinarians themselves, and when—in the event of any public procession of the Order—they march at the head of their Lodge, they handle the sword, and set and maintain the pace, as few civilians are able to do.

A very rare and noteworthy experience in connection with the subject of Past Masters acting as
unpaid Tylers may here be recorded.   The writer
was acting as Installing Master in a Lodge (not his
own) in which a Past Master had during several years
filled the Office of Tyler without fee or reward.   On
the anniversary in question, although he was so
seriously ill as to be forbidden to leave his bed, he
insisted upon going to the Lodge to be invested
once more with the Jewel of his Office.   A brother—
who was a medical man—saw him in the ante-room,
and said that if he were not quickly removed he
would probably die there.   He was led into the
Lodge, was invested with his Jewel with a brief
address, he saluted, and was led out again and immediately taken home.   Within two hours of that
time he died.

The duties defined in the address to the Tyler at
his Investiture, and partially repeated by the Junior
Warden in the opening of the Lodge in the First
Degree, are briefly these, 'That he is carefully to
guard every avenue of approach to the Lodge, so
that no cowan or unqualified intruder come within
sight or hearing of any of our mysteries; that he is
to exercise the strictest caution as to the admission
of visitors, and that he is to see that the Candidates
for the several Ceremonies come properly prepared.'

Of the first of these duties nothing need be said;
but our subject demands that some remarks be made
under the second head.   Upon the subject of the
admission of visitors the Tyler is cautioned that 'in
the event of a stranger professing to be a Freemason

seeking admission, he is immediately to summon the Junior Warden to his aid, so that the responsibility of either granting or refusing admission to the Lodge may not rest upon himself alone.' Etiquette, even ordinary politeness, requires that a probably well-qualified brother shall not be turned back simply upon the *ipse dixit* of the Tyler, but that one of the Principal Officers of the Lodge (that is, the Junior Warden) shall be the arbiter in such a case.

With regard to the third portion of the definition of the Tyler's duties, this will be mentioned when we treat of the preparation of Candidates in a future chapter.

In addition to the before-named duties of a Tyler, others of equal importance and indispensably necessary to the working of the Lodge, and to the convenience of the Officers and Brethren, come within the scope of his supervision. The furniture and implements, the collars and jewels, and, in short, all the belongings of the Lodge, are under his care, and he is responsible for their being kept always in good condition. He has to prepare the Lodge for all its meetings, and to see that everything that can be required in each Degree shall be in its proper place ready for use.

It may be asked, ' What has this description of the Tyler's multifarious duties to do with the Etiquette of Freemasonry?' We answer, ' Very much indeed.' One of the several meanings of the word etiquette, as may be seen on page 15, is, ' Forms which are observed in particular places.' This, more freely rendered, may be given as ' the right way in which to do the right thing, at the right time, and in the right place.' This applied to the work of the Lodge through the several Degrees will show that the duties of the Tyler, in the preparation of the Lodge, and in providing that everything that can possibly be wanted shall be in its proper place, have a very close connection with the subject of this treatise.

In addition to all the duties previously detailed, one more must be mentioned, namely, the duty of gaining an accurate knowledge of the preparation of the Candidates in each of the degrees, and of a thorough comprehension of the theory and practice of the K's upon the door. The word theory may well be applied to both these subjects, for one can seldom go wrong in the practice of either of them if one knows the reason why a certain form is practised at one time and not at another. These subjects will be discussed in the following chapter.

CHAPTER VIII.

Tyler to be assisted by D. of C. or a Deacon—Reasons for such assistance when Candidates are being prepared—The several Processes of Preparation explained—A rather gay Initiate— The White Feather—*Fiascos* to be avoided—The K.......s of the Three Degrees—May represent Standards of Value—Aid to Memory—'A Report' *v.* 'An Alarm' in each Degree fully explained—Admission of Strangers—The so-called 'Tyler's Obligation.'

ATTENTION may here be called to the desirability of the Director of Ceremonies (or in his absence one of the Deacons) leaving the Lodge and superintending— or, at least, inspecting before admission—the preparation of the Candidates in each Degree. The Tyler is liable to have his attention distracted by members or visitors coming or going, by having to answer the K's upon the door when the Lodge is being opened in the higher Degrees, and in many ways his thoughts may be diverted from the work in hand, and a mistake may be made in the preparation of the Candidate, however efficient generally the Tyler may be.

Another equally cogent reason may be given for the Tyler having the assistance of the Director of Ceremonies. In the preparation of a Candidate for the Ceremony of Initiation, there are certain processes which may well cause some surprise in the mind of a stranger ; in such a case—perhaps it would be well to say in all cases—it is desirable that the Director of Ceremonies, or the Deacon, should assure the Candidate that nothing is being done without a meaning ; that there is a good historical or traditional reason for every detail, and that in due time the whole will be explained, and will be made perfectly clear to him.

Probably some few of the Officers and Brethren who witness or assist at this preparation of a Candidate for Initiation, are themselves partially, or even totally, unaware of these reasons. In order that such of those as may read these pages may be instructed upon this subject, and that when in office they may be enabled to give the assurance contained in the previous paragraph with perfect truthfulness, a full explanation of the origin of, and the reasons for, the several processes of the preparation, derived from the Vol. of the S. L., and from tradition, is given in the Appendix E, page 242. These should be read with attention ; they could be committed to memory, wholly or partially, with very little study.

Two noteworthy incidents in connection with this subject recur to memory, and they are worth narrating in corroboration of our argument.

In the first case the Candidate, a rather gay, rollicking sort of man (a gentleman, nevertheless), treated the whole as a joke. A great deal of merriment—quite out of place in such a proceeding—had been allowed to go on unchecked in the ante-room. When the Candidate was conducted into the Lodge he made a profound obeisance, and with a great sweep of his right arm (he was a tall man with a loud voice), he said, 'Gentlemen, your most obedient.' As a matter of course, he was quickly turned out of the Lodge He was sharply rebuked for his misconduct; he saw that he had made a mistake, and gave a promise that nothing of the kind should occur again. He was re-admitted and duly initiated, and he afterwards proved to be a worthy and a thoroughly well-conducted member of the Lodge. This happened more than forty years ago.

The second case is of more recent date. The Candidate was a man of middle age. He cavilled and argued as the preparation went on, and when it came to the H....W....he positively refused to go farther. Possibly there had been a want of tact on the part of the Tyler; no one was there who could speak with authority, and could assure the candidate that not one thing was being done without a good reason, and that soon everything would be satisfactorily accounted for and fully explained. One of the Past Masters was called out, but in vain; the man was obstinate and he went away. It is extremely probable that in each of these cases, if an Officer of experience, possessing an ordinary amount of tact, and of powers of persuasion, had been present, these *fiascos* would not have occurred.

The next subject in connection with the duties of the Tyler which demands our attention is the series of K......s upon the door. Either from carelessness or from an innate maladroitness, the K......s are too often jumbled, or so imperfectly sounded as to necessitate correction, which to a great extent interferes with the smooth and correct working of the Lodge. The K......s severally of the three Degrees are simple in the extreme, and when the theory of their arrangement is once understood, a mistake need never be made in giving them.

Let us imagine that the K......s of the First Degree represent a certain standard of value, and that those of the Second Degree are of higher value, and those of the Third Degree are higher still. To illustrate this theory we may compare them with coins of the realm. In this view the K......s of the First Degree will be represented by *the regulaticn number* of *pence;* those of the Second Degree, rising in value, will be represented by one shilling and the requisite number of pence, and those of the Third Degree, still rising in value, will be equal to two shillings, and the remainder in the lower coinage.

This is an old system, in frequent use forty years ago, and anyone repeating the formula aloud, will find that it quickly fixes itself upon the memory, and when so fixed it will never be forgotten. This plan will be found extremely useful to young members, and indeed to all who need an aid to memory in this direction.

It is, however, in the K......s upon the door, which signify severally 'a report' and 'an alarm' in each Degree, that the worst confusion is generally to be found. We will here endeavour to give a clear explanation of the difference between 'a report' and 'an alarm.' 'A report' consists of the K......s of the Degree in which the Lodge may happen to be, and which the Tyler gives to intimate that a member of the Lodge, or a properly qualified visitor, seeks admission. 'An alarm' is sounded by a K.....k, or a series of K.......s, *which differ from those of the Degree*

in which the Lodge is open at the time, and by which
the Brethren within are given to understand that the
Candidate waits seeking admission, or in the improbable, but just possible, case of a cowan, or a
stranger professing to be a Freemason, endeavouring
to force his way into the Lodge.

We will now explain more fully, first 'the report.'
When the Lodge is open in the First Degree, and a
member, or a well-known Brother, seeks admission, the
K......s of the Degree are given, that is, those of the
lowest denomination in value. In the Second Degree, for
a member or a visitor who is known to have taken that
Degree, the K......s of the next higher denomination
are given by the Tyler, and in the Third Degree those
of the highest value are given. In each and in all of
these cases the K......s so given, being respectively
the K......s of the Degree in which the Lodge is
opened at that particular time, constitute '*a report.*'

We will now consider 'the alarm' in each Degree.
When a Candidate for Initiation is conducted to the
door the K......s of the First Degree must not be
given by the Tyler, for two reasons. Firstly, the
Candidate should not be allowed to become acquainted with the regular K......s until after his
Initiation is completed; and secondly, the Brethren
within the Lodge have to be warned that a stranger
(that is, one who is not a Freemason) stands outside
the door. For these reasons a K.....k should be given
which shall be totally different from the K......s of the
First Degree; therefore one tolerably loud K.....k is
sounded on the door, and that constitutes 'an alarm,'
clear and unmistakable.

When a Candidate for passing is brought to the door, the Lodge being at that time opened in the Second Degree, the K......s of that Degree should not be given, for the same reasons as those before stated, namely, that the Candidate should not be allowed to become acquainted with the K......s until the Ceremony of Passing is completed, and in order that the Brethren within the Lodge may be warned that one who is not a Fellow-Craft is seeking admission. Therefore a K.....k differing from that of the Second Degree should be given; and inasmuch as the Candidate is then fully acquainted with the K......s of the First Degree, it is right and proper that those K......s should be given, and when so given, differing as they do from those of the then Degree, they constitute ' an alarm,' at the same time conveying to those in the Lodge not that a stranger, but that an Entered Apprentice seeks admission.

The same reasons exactly apply to the Third Degree; the Candidate must not be allowed to gain prematurely a knowledge of the K......s of the then Degree, and the Brethren within the Lodge have to be informed that the Candidate (necessarily a Fellow-Craft) seeks admission; therefore the K......s of the Second Degree are given, and they serve as ' an alarm.'

In brief, to sound ' an alarm ' for a Candidate in the First Degree, one distinct K.....k is given; for a Candidate in the Second Degree, the K......s of an Entered Apprentice; and for a Candidate in the Third Degree, the K......s of a Fellow-Craft are given. In each Degree, the K.....k or K......s given being different from those of the Degree in which the Lodge is opened at the time, the Officers and Brethren are made aware that a Candidate seeks admission; and the Inner Guard is enabled at once to use the word 'alarm' in his announcement to the Junior Warden, and the Junior Warden does the same in sending the message on to the Worshipful Master.

A custom appears to prevail in the United States of admitting strangers who profess to be Freemasons, but who have no friend or acquaintance to vouch for them, who have with them no certificate, and who apparently are subjected to little or no examination, but who nevertheless are received into the Lodge upon taking that which they call the Tyler's obligation. This is, in plain English, the meaning of the words in italics in the following extract from Bro. Dr. Mackey's Masonic Law. The words mentioned being capable of being thus paraphrased: '... they may still be admitted by the production of their certificate, or by an examination as to their knowledge of Freemasonry; or, dispensing with both these safeguards, they may be admitted by the Tyler's obligation.' A very loose and reprehensible custom, which we may devoutly hope may never be imported into this country. The extract runs thus:

'But many brethren who are desirous of visiting are strangers and sojourners, without either friends or acquaintances amongst the members to become their vouchers; in which case they may still be admitted *by certificate, examination, or the aid of the sacred volume*, commonly called the Tyler's obligation, which, in the United States, runs in the following form : " I, A.B., do hereby and hereon solemnly and sincerely swear that I have been regularly initiated, passed, and raised to the sublime degree of a Master Mason in a just and legally constituted Lodge ; that I do not stand suspended or expelled, and know of no reason why I should not hold Masonic communication with my Brethren." ' The doctor concludes with the dictum, ' And this is all that Freemasonry needs to provide !' We in England think this is not *all* by a very long way.

CHAPTER IX.

DIVERSITIES IN THE OPENINGS AND CLOSINGS.

Customs of a Locality or of a Province—Again, 'Mason' or
'Freemason'?—The Legitimate and Original Appellation—
Freemasonry a Progressive Science—*Seeing* and *Proving*—
Indications of a Difference in Procedure—Evidence of an
early Ritual—The course of the Sun in relation to the
Principal Officers.

IN the opening and the closing of the Lodge in the
several Degrees, although a general similarity exists,
yet there are distinct diversities in some details. For
instance, in a Lodge in one of the home counties one
K.....k is given to announce a Member or a well-
known visitor, whatever the Degree in which the
Lodge may be at the time; while for a Candidate in
either Degree the K......s of that Degree are always
given. This may be the custom of the locality, or of
the Province. No matter how general it may be, it is
diametrically opposed to the rule laid down in the
last chapter, and that is the common-sense rule.

We will here notice some observances of more or
less importance which are not included in the actual
Ritual, but which are essential to the correct and
harmonious working of the Lodge. We have in
Chapter II. of this work discussed at some length the
appellation of our Order, and of ourselves as Mem-

bers of the Order ; we refer to this question here because it is forced upon our attention in the first words which the Worshipful Master addresses to the Junior Warden, namely, ' ... what is the first care of every ' ... what shall it be, ' Mason or Freemason ' ? One of the chief publications devoted to the interests of the Craft is *The Freemason.* Would this organ of our Order commend itself to the notice of Brethren if its title were *The Mason ?* Again, the head-quarters of our organization in London is ' Free-masons' Hall.' Would Grand Lodge submit to its being called ' Masons' Hall ' ? Emphatically *no.*

It may be said, ' This question is one of Ritual ;' true, but it lies well within the domain of Etiquette at the same time. In the outer world we do not deny to men the titles of honour to which they have an undisputed right. We do not salute a Prince or a Peer as Sir John ; we do not call a Baronet or a Knight Mr. Jones or Mr. Smith ; we do not call a Barrister a Solicitor, or a Physician an Apothecary or a Druggist ; it would be contrary to etiquette to do so ; therefore we assert and maintain that the ' Etiquette of Free-masonry requires that we call each other Freemasons, and our Order Freemasonry.'

It follows, therefore, that the first question in the opening of the Lodge should be, ' Bro. Junior Warden, what is the first care of every *Free-mason ?*' and that, when the Senior Warden is next addressed, his answer should be, ' To see that none but *Freemasons* are present.' Similarly when the Inner Guard is called upon to define his duty, his answer should be, ' To admit *Freemasons* upon proof,

etc. . .' and so on through every portion of the
opening and closing in each Degree, and in each
Ceremony. Consistency requires this, for it is
inconsistent in the extreme to ask in the First Degree,
' ...what is the first care of every *Mason ?*' and that the
corresponding question in the opening in the Second
Degree should be, ' ....what is the first care of
every Fellow-Craft *Freemason ?*' because we are as
fully, as clearly, as incontestably, Freemasons in the
First Degree, as we are in the Second ; and there is
no reason why the one designation (the correct one)
should not be used in each case alike. Why should
our pure and noble *Science* be degraded in name to
the level of a mere mechanical *business ?* Besides
this, there is the inconsistency, which is to be seen in
all the older Rituals, and in most of the works upon
Freemasonry, namely the free and indiscriminate use
of, sometimes Mason and Masonry, sometimes Freemasons and Freemasonry. The opposing words
being found mixed and jumbled, here and there, and
often in the same paragraph, without rhyme or reason.
Good sense, propriety, etiquette, are all on the side
of the *restoration* of the legitimate appellation of our
Order ; the *original* appellation, as is clearly proved
in the historical record given on pages 26-28.

While following, more or less closely, the opening
and closing of the Lodge, and the work of the three
Ceremonies, it will be necessary not only to mention
certain things which should be done, or said, but
also to point out many curious, some obsolete, some
altogether indefensible, customs ; the greater number
of them possibly local in their origin and use. We

6

may also occasionally advert to certain customs, observances, and forms of words, which may be considered to be superior to those in more general use, and to be therefore worthy of adoption. We should never cease to bear in mind the sentence in the Second Degree, in which the Candidate is told that 'Freemasonry is a *progressive* Science;' the progress here intended being necessarily progressive improvement.

In many well-worked Lodges, in more than one Province, it is the invariable custom, in the opening of the Lodge in each of the three Degrees, when the Inner Guard receives the instruction from the Junior Warden to '*see* that the Lodge is properly Tyled,' for him (the Inner Guard) to open the door, and actually to *see* that the Tyler is in his place. Much may be urged in favour of this custom. The Inner Guard does precisely, and literally, that which he is ordered to do. He is told to *see*, etc. ; he opens the door and *sees*. On the other hand, in the closing, the Junior Warden instructs the Inner Guard to *prove*, etc., so he gives the K......s and thus *proves*, etc. Another reason may be given. In the first questions which the Worshipful Master addresses to the Junior and the Senior Warden, respectively, he calls each of them by his proper name, and not by the name of his Office ; and in their replies they each address the Master by his own name. The reason for this is clearly that the brethren present have not yet proved themselves to be Freemasons, and therefore that a possible cowan may not be allowed to learn the titles of the Officers. By the same rule in the opening in each Degree, before the brethren present have proved themselves, the K......k of the then Degree is not given upon the door, lest it should improperly become known to the problematical cowan ; therefore the door is silently opened, and the Lodge in each Degree is *seen* to be properly Tyled. The fact of the difference in the wording, between the command in the opening and the corresponding order in the closing, seems to point to a difference in procedure.

The difference, so clearly marked, between the order given in the opening and the one given in the closing, is strong presumptive evidence that the custom in earlier times corresponded with that just described, namely, that the Inner Guard, when instructed by the Junior Warden to ' *see* that the Lodge was properly Tyled,' did open the door and *see ;* and that when ordered to '*prove* that the Lodge was close Tyled,' he *proved* the fact by the regular K......s in each Degree.

In corroboration of this presumption, we may take the evidence of a very early copy of the Ritual in the possession of the writer. The passage runs thus : ' The I. G., after *seeing* that the Tyler is in his proper place, turns round, and says to the J. W., "Brother A. B. (name), the Lodge is properly Tyled."' In the opening in the Second Degree, and in the Third, the words are precisely the same, *i.e.*, ' after *seeing*.' In the closing in each of the three Degrees the words are : ' The I. G. gives the K...,...s, which are answered by the Tyler ;' thus showing that no accident or carelessness had caused the differences in the orders given respectively in the openings and the closings, because they are *each three time repeated*, and always respectively in the same form of words.

The Ritual from which these quotations are taken has unfortunately lost the title-page, and with it the date of publication. It is unlike in size, and type, and manner of construction, any Ritual known to the writer. It is not Carlile's nor Claret's, certainly ; it is more grammatical and generally correct than either of these. It is very dilapidated, worn with years of use, and the leaves are yellow with age. It is presumably a very rare copy.

Another custom connected with the opening of the Lodge in the First Degree may here be noted. We will premise that in every Lodge the question asked of the Junior Warden by the Worshipful Master, 'Why are you so placed?' is answered in some such words as this : 'To mark the sun at its meridian,' etc. And when a similar question is addressed to the Senior Warden, he answers : 'To mark the setting sun,' etc. In the Lodges whose usage in this respect we are considering, when the Master asks, 'Why is he (the Master) placed in the east?' the Past Master answers, 'To represent the rising sun ; for as the sun rises in the east,' etc. This is far less abrupt, and it forms a more complete and consistent explanation of the reason why, than to say briefly, 'As the sun rises in the east,' etc.

Furthermore, the statement that the Worshipful Master is placed in the east to represent the rising sun, agreeing as it does ·in this respect with the answers given by the Junior and the Senior Wardens, carries the allusion to 'that grand luminary of nature and centre of our system,' through the three phases of its course: the rising, the attainment of its meridian altitude, and its setting, and identifies each of those periods with the position respectively of the three principal Officers of the Lodge.

This reply sounds well in the Lodge, as it does also in the address to the Worshipful Master after his Installation, when the Installing Master says: 'You are now placed in the east to represent the rising sun, and as a pattern for your imitation I would refer you to,' etc.

The instances thus quoted may be considered steps on the way of progressive improvement, therefore the right way to do the right thing, and consequently quite consistent with etiquette, in the broad acceptation of the word.

CHAPTER X.

THE CHAPLAIN AND HIS DUTIES.

Desirable that every Lodge should have a Chaplain—It en-
hances the Impressiveness and Solemnity of the Proceedings
—Services required of the Chaplain—His Place in the Lodge
—Slight change necessary in the Opening—Attitude of the
Brethren during Prayer—A Purely Secular Declaration—The
Reductio ad absurdum—A Question far above the Sphere of
Ritual—'So mote it be '—The practice of chanting the words
—It seems that all may join in the Response.

IT is highly desirable that a Chaplain should be
appointed in every Lodge which has among its
members a duly qualified brother; and, as a matter
of course, that all the devotional portions of the opening and the closing in each Degree, and in each of
the three Ceremonies, should be performed by him.
The impressiveness and the solemnity of the whole
proceedings are materially enhanced by having a
Chaplain to perform those important duties.

The address delivered to the Chaplain at his investiture, on·the day of Installation, gives a very clear
explanation of the services required to be rendered by
him as follows :

CHAPLAIN.

' Bro. ......, I have the honour to invest you as
Chaplain of this Lodge. Your Jewel, the Open

Book, represents the Volume of the Sacred Law, which is always open upon the Master's Pedestal when the Brethren are at labour in the Lodge. The V. of the S. L. is the greatest of the three greater lights in Freemasonry; by its teaching we are instructed to rule and guide our faith and our actions. Without it the Lodge is not perfect, and without an openly avowed belief in its Divine Author, no Candidate can be lawfully initiated into our Order. Your place in the Lodge is on the right of the Worshipful Master, and as, both in the opening and the closing of the Lodge in each Degree, as well as in each of the three Ceremonies, the blessing of the Almighty is invoked in aid of our proceedings, it will be your duty, as far as may be possible, to attend all the meetings of the Lodge, in order that you may exercise your sacred office in the devotional portions of our Ceremonies.'

In an earlier chapter mention is made of the place which the Chaplain should occupy in the Lodge, and a suggestion is made that he should have a seat upon the daïs. His sacerdotal office seems to demand that his position in the Lodge should be raised above the level of the brethren generally.

When the Chaplain performs his duty in the opening of the Lodge in the First Degree, a very slight change in the wording is indispensable, namely, the transfer of a few words, usually uttered by the Master, to the Chaplain, thus: 'Chaplain: Brethren, the Lodge being thus duly formed, before the Worshipful Master declares it open, let us invoke a blessing, etc. . . .'

During the prayer, all the Brethren (including the Worshipful Master, and the Chaplain himself) stand in the attitude of devotion; this is universally practised. It is mentioned here in order to direct attention to the desirability of the Brethren assuming the attitude *simultaneously*, and of dropping it in the same manner. For this purpose, they should look to the Worshipful Master and the Director of Ceremonies, and should keep time with their movements.

One cannot help noticing that, for a time after the conclusion of the prayer, many of the Brethren retain the position, quite unconsciously, while others have very properly altered theirs at the right moment. This is unseemly; Brethren will do well to bear in mind that all things should be done decently and *in order*.

With the close of the prayer, the devotional portion of the opening of the Lodge is concluded. We venture, therefore, to suggest that the Worshipful Master has no need, and, indeed, no right, to use the name of T. G. A. O. T. U. in the sentence in which he declares the Lodge open. The sentence contains not even a suggestion of invocation, of prayer, or of praise; it is a purely secular declaration, it acquires no force or additional meaning from the use of the Sacred Name.

We may well ask by what authority the Master assumes the right to speak in the name of the Almighty? Logically, it means, ' I, speaking in the name—that is, as the representative—of T. G. A. O. T. U., declare,' etc. And what does he declare? It is no message of high import, as befits the representative of the Almighty, or one who speaks in His

Name. There is in it no spiritual teaching, no moral lesson, but simply a declaration that the Lodge is opened for ordinary business—a simple, commonplace ending to so pretentious a beginning.

If we question—as we seriously do—the right of the Worshipful Master to arrogate to himself the authority to speak in that Great and Holy Name, what shall we say of the assumption by the Senior Warden of the same authority, when he uses that Name in the investiture of the Candidates in each Degree? We may go farther, and ask why this should stop in its downward course, and why the Inner Guard should not assert an equal right, and say, 'Brother Junior Warden, in the Name of T. G. A. O. T. U. the Lodge is properly Tyled'? This, of course, is the *reductio ad absurdum*, but it is not beyond the bounds of fair argument, for the act of putting on an apron has no more connection, near or remote, with the Divine Name, than has the closing of the door. One almost hesitates to compare this misuse of the Sacred Name with the oft-quoted case of the Oriental vendor of figs, whose constant cry in the streets of Bagdad was, ' In the name of the Prophet—Figs !'

' Sic parvis componere magna, solebam.'

This question rises far above the sphere of Ritual and etiquette ; far above custom or tradition, even if the *authenticity* of the tradition could be proved ; it is a question of reverence for the Creator, and for His commandment, which forbids us to take ' His Name in vain.'

The following excerpt from ' The Revised Ritual '

expresses all that further needs to be said upon this subject.

'A bad old custom exists in many Lodges, where, in opening the Lodge in each Degree, the W. M. says : "I. T. N. O. T. G. A. O. T. U., I declare the Lodge duly opened ;" or in the Second Degree. "J. T. N. O. T. G. G. O. T. U. ;" or in the Third Degree, "I. T. N. O. T. M. H.," using the same invocation (desecration, rather) in the closing, and in the investiture of the Candidate in each Degree. This is a remnant of the time when wills and other legal documents began with the formula—"In the name of God, Amen ;" and when men thoughtlessly used the words " Good God !" or " My God !" to express surprise. No will or other legal deed now has the above form of words, and no man of education or refinement exclaims "Good God !" or " My God !" upon every light occasion. The better sense of mankind has awakened to the fact that such expressions are distinctly "taking God's name in vain,' and a direct breach of the third commandment. In our Lodges we open and close in each Degree with "solemn prayer," and each Ceremony is commenced with prayer ; this is correct and appropriate. In the Charge the Candidate is exhorted never to mention God's name " but with the awe and reverence which are due from the creature to his Creator ;" then, surely, we should in all our Lodges discontinue the use of a form of words quite superfluous, if not profane, and devoid of "the awe and reverence ' inculcated in the Charge."

'Liberavi animam meam.'

One other subject connected with the opening and closing of the Lodge may well be discussed in this place, namely, Is it etiquette for one or more or the whole of the Brethren present to pronounce the words ' So mote it be '? Opinions and practice differ upon the subject. It is held in certain Lodges that the Immediate Past Master *alone* has the right to use the words ; in others, that the right belongs to the whole of the Past Masters, and to none below that rank. This was the practice in Oxford forty years ago, giving rise to the irreverent allusion to a Past Master as a ' *Mote it be* '! Undergraduates *of that day* were not distinguished by an excessive development of the organ of Reverence. The practice in many Lodges is for the whole of the brethren to join in the repetition of the words.

There is no authoritative pronouncement upon the subject, therefore we must expect to find differences in practice in different Lodges. Taking the words in their literal meaning, they will be found to be synonymous with the word Amen (So be it), which is in universal use at the end of every prayer, public or private. In public the prayer recited by Priest or Minister is adopted by every member of the congregation by the use of the word Amen ; so by a parity of reasoning we may say that the several prayers recited by the Chaplain in the Lodge are adopted by *every member* present by the utterance of the words ' So mote it be.'

If the parallel thus drawn is held to be good reasoning, it follows that as in a congregation of worshippers everyone present has the right to utter the word Amen, so in a Lodge every member present has full liberty to use the words ' So mote it be.'

Where this formula is chanted, as a matter of course all join in the chant—at least, they are entitled to do so—and that which may be sung by all, may surely be said by all without distinction.

The practice of chanting the words in question is not universal ; it is perhaps not as general as it deserves to be. When accompanied by the organ or the harmonium, the effect is infinitely more impressive than the spoken words can possibly be. It is much to be desired that this portion at least of the Ceremonies should be musical.

In the Programme of the Consecration of a new Lodge quite recently, where the Consecrating Officer was a high dignitary of Grand Lodge, and the acting Wardens, the Tyler, and the Directors of Ceremonies were all past or present Grand Officers of high rank, after every prayer came the line ' Chant (Omnes), So mote it be.' This may be taken, not only as an example to be followed, but as, in fact, authorizing the practice and establishing a precedent.*

* See ' Consecration of a Lodge,' pages 223-230.

CHAPTER XI

OBSERVANCES IN THE OPENINGS.

Two Divergences in the Fellow-Craft—Signs too literally and fully given—The I. P. M. and the Compasses—Standing to Order as a Fellow-Craft—Peculiarity of Certain Questions—Proving by Signs—Exaggeration of Gesture to be avoided—An Illustrative and Amusing Anecdote—Taking the Time so that all should be in Unison—Repetition of Titles tedious and unnecessary—A Curious Answer—*Why* and *Because*—Note when the Chaplain recites the Prayer — A Curious Custom.

LITTLE variation exists in the form of the opening in the Second Degree. The use of the title Fellow-Craft Freemason is happily universal. Two divergences may, however, occasionally—but rarely—be noticed. One sometimes hears the Worshipful Master address the Junior Warden thus: '...... you will prove the Brethren to be Craftsmen *by s....s....*' The use of the words 'by s....s' is incorrect. The Candidate in the Second Degree is instructed that 'the s... in this Degree is t... f..., or may be separated into t... several s...s.' In proving themselves to be Craftsmen the Brethren do not, or rather should not, adopt the separate forms of the s... seriatim; but by a simultaneous movement should place themselves at once in the proper position, and that is sufficient proof.

It is unfortunately a fact that in some country

Lodges, where the order is given to the brethren to prove themselves by s ...s, they do so literally and fully.

The second error to be noticed is this : the Worshipful Master commences his declaration by saying, 'Brethren, the Lodge being *thus duly formed* before I declare it open in the Second Degree.' This is altogether a mistake; the Lodge is 'duly formed' once and for all in the opening in the First Degree, by the naming of the several Officers, principal and subordinate, and by the description of their respective positions and their individual duties. The Degrees differ, and each Degree requires a separate opening, but it is one Lodge throughout. The correct form is the one in general use. The Master or the Chaplain says, 'Brethren, before the Lodge is opened in the Second Degree, let us supplicate,' etc.

After the Prayer it is generally understood that the Immediate Past Master, or one acting for him, descends from the daïs and alters the relative positions of the points of the C... upon the Volume of the Sacred Law. This remark applies to the opening and the closing in each of the three Degrees.

We mentioned in a previous paragraph that in proving themselves to be Fellow-Craft Freemasons, the Brethren should, 'by a simultaneous movement, place themselves at once in the proper position.' This was sufficiently accurate as a general direction, but in fact the strict rule is to place the right hand in position just the smallest instant of time before the left is raised. When, however, the Worshipful Master declares 'the Lodge duly opened upon the Square,' the order is reversed : the left hand is lowered at the word 'Square,' and then at the end of the sentence the third portion of the three-fold s... may be given with the right hand in the act of removing it from its position.

Thus we have two movements, almost, but not quite, synchronous, in the act of standing to order, and two movements with a short interval between in dropping the s....

It will have been noticed that in opening the Lodge in the Second and in the Third Degrees, the first question asked is couched in terms relating to the Degree in which the Lodge is about to be opened, and not to the Degree in which the Lodge stands at the time. Thus in opening in the Second Degree the question runs thus, 'Brother Junior Warden, what is the first care of every Fellow-Craft Freemason?' although the Lodge is at the moment open only in the First or Entered Apprentices' Degree. Similarly, in opening in the Third Degree the question is, 'Brother Junior Warden, what is the first care of every Master Mason?' the Lodge at the time being in the Second or Fellow-Crafts' Degree. There should be no departure from this rule; it should be universally practised; but unfortunately instances of laxity in this respect are of not infrequent occurrence.

During the opening in the Third Degree, the command to the Brethren to 'prove themselves to be Master Masons *by s...s*' is quite correct; the Brethren do so literally, by making consecutively the three ordinary s...s of a Master Mason. There is no evolution, in the whole range of ceremonial observances in the Lodge, in which so many and so wide divergences from the correct forms are to be seen, as in the making of these three s...s, more especially in the first. This s... cannot, of course, be described; we can only suggest that all the movements of the body and the limbs should be made with freedom of action, and should be fully developed, but at the same time with *no exaggeration of gesture.* The proper movements and position, once acquired, are perfectly easy, and are never forgotten.

An old memory recurs to the writer's mind in illustration of the argument against exaggeration of gesture. In a Lodge of which he was a member many years ago, an old Past Master (Bro. S...) was distinguished for being always excessively demonstrative in making the several s...s, and more particularly the first of the Third Degree. In the course of time another Past Master, previously a member of a Lodge in another Province, was admitted as a joining member of the Lodge in which Bro. S... was a Past Master, and the first time the Lodge was opened in the Third Degree in the presence of the joining member, it was seen that the older member was nowhere, in the way of exaggeration of gesture, in comparison with Bro. B..., the new arrival, of whom it was said that 'he flung his arms about like the sails of a windmill.' Bro. S... witnessed Bro. B...'s performance once, and no more; he never entered the Lodge again. It was suggested that he saw that there was not sufficient floor space in the Lodge for him and Bro. B... to exhibit the full s...s of a Master Mason in the same room at the same time. They were both tall, long-armed, loose-limbed, angular men. They had either forgotten, or they had never taken to themselves, Hamlet's advice to the players, 'Suit the action to the word, the word to the action, with this special observance, that you *o'er-step not the modesty of nature.*'

Whenever the Brethren are commanded to stand to order in either Degree, it is well for them *to look* (*not to turn*) to the East, so that they may keep time accurately with the Worshipful Master and the Director of Ceremonies ; and when the period of standing to order is past—still looking to the East—all should drop the s... at the same moment with the Worshipful Master. The same rule applies to the position assumed by all present during the several devotional portions of the Ceremonies. All should look to the East, and all should move together.

When the Brethren are commanded to prove themselves in the opening in the Second and the Third Degrees, they should look to the West, and should take their time from the Senior Warden. In many Lodges, after the command itself, the Junior Warden adds, 'looking to the West,' or, better still, 'taking your time from the Senior Warden.' The object all through is to get the Brethren to make every movement in unison. This can be done only by taking the time from one man. Perhaps the best example of discipline in this respect is to be found in military Lodges. The perfection of accuracy and precision of movement and of time are, of course, to be expected from these drilled and trained men ; these qualities, however, are not difficult in practice in private Lodges : the habit is easily acquired, but unfortunately so many of the Brethren, as it were, fight for their own hand, and do not strive after combined and simultaneous action. Every Brother should visit a Military Lodge if one such happen to be held 'within the length of his cable-tow,' and he will see how charming and instructive such a visit will be ; 'profit and pleasure will be the result,' to a certainty.

After the Brethren have proved themselves in the Third Degree, the Worshipful Master says, ' Brother Junior Warden, whence come,' etc. ; and on receiving the reply he says, 'Brother Senior Warden, whither directing,' etc. The whole of the following questions may be given alternately, without prefacing each with ' Brother Junior Warden ' or ' Brother Senior Warden.' The reiteration of the respective titles becomes tedious, and it is unnecessary. Each of the Wardens knows, or ought to know, which question comes next, and which of them will have to answer it. If he does not know this, he should keep his eyes fixed upon the Worshipful Master, who will so address each question to each Warden in turn that no mistake can be made and no delay can ensue.

The last answer in the opening in the Third Degree, made by the Senior Warden in many Lodges, and as it stands in some of the published Rituals, namely, ' *That being* a point from which no Master Mason can materially err ' is a very curious one : it is inchoate and incomplete. In order to make it a complete and grammatical sentence it might run thus : ' That being a point from which no Master Mason can materially err, *we naturally look for the G. S. of a M. M. upon the C....*' The answer given in certain Lodges, and as it stands in the Revised Ritual and in the old Ritual mentioned on page 83, runs thus : ' *Because* that is a point from which a Master Mason cannot materially err.' This sentence is brief, complete, and conclusive.

If one were walking or driving with a friend and he took a sharp turn to the right or to the left, and his friend asked him why he 'did not keep on the high-road,' one would not say, ' *That* (or, rather, *this*) *being* the way to our destination.' No, he would reply in the ordinary way, thus, ' *Because* this is the way to our destination.' It may be safely predicated that in almost every case when a question begins with the word 'Why,' the answer begins with the word 'Because.' It is common-sense and plain English.

If the Chaplain recites the Prayer, he must follow the Worshipful Master in this manner :

W. M.—Then, Brethren, we will assist you to repair that loss.

CHAPLAIN.—And may the blessing of the M. H. rest upon our united endeavours.

CHANT (OMNES).—So mote it be.

When the Worshipful Master declares the Lodge duly opened upon the centre, he and all the Brethren should draw the right hand *sharply* from its position and drop it to the side, all in perfect unison.

(*In some Lodges, the Worshipful Master alone first gives the G. and R. S., next the Worshipful Master and Senior Warden, and thirdly the Worshipful Master, the Wardens, and the whole of the Brethren. The words accompany the s... in each case ; that is, they are spoken first by the Worshipful Master alone, then by the Worshipful Master and the Senior Warden together, and thirdly by all together.*)

This is mentioned rather as a curious custom than as being desirable as an example to be followed.

CHAPTER XII.

OBSERVANCES IN THE CLOSINGS.

Diversities of Practice—Wording of Certain Questions—Peculia.
Phraseology—A Slight Change desirable—'World' *versus*
'Universe'—Two Points to be noticed—'To whom does it
allude?'—'As happily we have met'—'Has every Brother
had his Due?'—Three Forms of the Closing Prayer—Proper
Form of Closing—A Solemn and Impressive Ending—Closing
summarily by Authority—Superfluous Additions—Calling
from Labour to Refreshment, and *vice versâ*—High Time and
High Noon—Breaches of Orthography and Etiquette.

COMPARATIVELY little needs to be said upon the subject of the closing of the Lodge in the three Degrees;
still, there are diversities of practice, good, bad, or in-
different, which may well be mentioned.

Everyone knows, or ought to know, that the wording
of the first question addressed to the Junior Warden
in the closing in each Degree differs from the somewhat similar question which occurs in the opening,
and that the several answers differ also in accordance
with the different wording of the questions. Thus,
in the closing in each Degree, the instruction given to
the Inner Guard is, 'To *prove* the Lodge *close* tyled,'
and he accordingly *proves* it in the established form
and manner. This question has been fully discussed
on page 82, to which it would be well to refer.

In the closing in the Third Degree, after the s...s

have been 'regularly communicated' and the Worshipful Master resumes his place, he makes a certain declaration. In the sentence then spoken one often hears a sad jumble, the result of running one sentence into the other. In fact, it is often rendered unintelligible for want of correct punctuation and a clear separation of the two parts of the sentence. It is no uncommon occurrence to hear it spoken thus, '...... the humble representative of K. S. do sanction, and confirm, and declare'—all this without a pause, leading one to conclude that the speaker himself has but a hazy idea of the meaning.

The truth is, the phraseology of this sentence is peculiar. This peculiarity is to be noticed in other parts of the Ritual; it is in the placing of the accusative case before the nominative and the verb. The same form of construction will be found in the Obligation in each Degree, in the words, 'These several points I solemnly swear to observe,' etc. In ordinary colloquial English we should say, 'I solemnly swear to observe these several points;' but in this latter form we should lose very much in emphasis and force of expression. The older form is by far the better form *for us*.

In like manner, if the declaration of the Worshipful Master upon the subject of the s...s were rendered into ordinary English, it would read thus :

'Brethren, as the Master of this Lodge, and thereby the humble representative of King Solomon, I sanction and confirm the substituted S... of a M. M. which have been thus regularly communicated to me : and I hereby declare that they shall serve to distinguish you, and all Master Masons throughout the world (*not universe*), until time or circumstances shall restore the genuine ones.'

We may put it in a more authoritative form, thus: 'Brethren, I, as the Master of this Lodge, and thereby the humble representative of K... S..., sanction and confirm the substituted S...,' etc.

We would, however, none of us desire to have the sentence thus transposed or used in the Lodge in any new form. The old construction of the sentence has become archaic; it may almost rank as a Landmark, which it would be a crime to attempt to remove. The right thing to do is to retain the form of construction, and the very words, but at the same time to render the passage clear and intelligible beyond the possibility of misunderstanding the full meaning. If we add a semicolon after the word 'confirm,' and insert the personal pronoun 'I' after the word 'and,' the whole meaning becomes perfectly clear. With this slight change the whole sentence will read thus:

W. M.—'Brethren, the substituted S...s of a Master Mason, which have been thus regularly communicated to me, I, as the Master of this Lodge, and thereby the humble representative of King Solomon, do sanction and confirm; and *I* hereby declare that they shall serve to distinguish you, and all Master Masons throughout the world, until time or circumstances shall restore the genuine ones.'

No *reasonable* objection can be made to this slight change; on the contrary, every thoughtful and educated Member of the Craft must acknowledge the reasonableness of our contention.

In certain Rituals we find the word 'universe' in this sentence. This is a gross error and an absurdity. We have no means of ascertaining whether Freemasonry is practised in any of the countless *worlds* in the *universe* other than our own; and if we had a certain knowledge that it is so practised it is probable that an edict, promulgated by the sovereign of a small portion of this earth's surface, would not have much effect in those other worlds, near and far, which make up the universe. Surely the perpetuation of the use of the word 'universe' in this sentence is not one of the Landmarks.

The closing in the Second Degree calls for little remark. Just two points may be noticed. The question, 'To Whom does it allude?' is sometimes answered thus, ' *To God*, T. G. G. O. T. U.' This is incorrect; it will be found that the word 'God' does not occur once in the whole of the three Ceremonies, except in the Obligation of an Entered Apprentice, and in the Charge in the First Degree, and in one other place in the Ceremony of Initiation. An explanation of its use in that place will be given in a future chapter. In each Degree a distinct name or title, embodying an attribute, or an ascription of power to the Almighty, is used throughout. Thus we have in the First Degree, T. G. A. O. T. U. ; in the Second, T. G. G. O. T. U., and in the Third T. M. H. Consequently there is no more justification, or need, to use the Sacred Name in the Second Degree than there is in the First or the Third. It is, moreover, a superfluity; it gives no more power or meaning to the sentence than is possessed by the words T. G. G. O. T. U.

At the end of the closing the Junior Warden is often heard to utter this formula :

> ' Happy have we met,
> Happy may we part,
> And happy meet again.'

To meet '*happy*,' to part '*happy*,' and to meet again '*happy*' does not seem to be in strict accordance with the rules of grammar. A similar formula is in use in certain Lodges ; it runs thus :

> ' As happily we have met,
> And happy we have been ;
> So happily may we part,
> And happily meet again.'

This has the merit of being at once grammatical and metrical.

In the general closing of the Lodge a curious custom exists in some well-worked Lodges in which, after the Senior Warden has named his place in the Lodge and has spoken the words, ' ... after having seen that every Brother has had his due,' the following question is addressed to him :

W. M.—' Has every Brother had his due ?'

S. W.—' All, except the Outer Guard or Tyler, and I will see that he is duly attended to.'

No doubt this form is of ancient date and usage in the locality in which it is practised ; it probably does not prevail over a wide area. This practice is mentioned simply as a curiosity, and not as an example to be extensively followed ; nevertheless it is entirely unobjectionable, and it has a flavour of antiquity about it.

The closing Prayer is variously worded in different

Lodges and Rituals. We will give three examples :
' ... may He continue to preserve *the* Order by
cementing and adorning *it* with every moral and
social virtue.' The old Ritual, mentioned on page
83, has the clause in this form : ' ... may He continue
to preserve *our* Order by beautifying and adorning *us*
with every moral and social virtue.'

It would certainly seem that the 'moral and social
virtues' belong in an especial sense to the Members
rather than to the Order. The same view is embodied
in the third example, which we here give in full.
' Brethren, before the Lodge is closed, let us with all
reverence and humility express our gratitude to T. G.
A. O. T. U. for the favours which we have received,
and may He continue to preserve our Order by
adorning its Members with every moral and social
virtue.'

It will probably be held that the latter form is the
better worded. It sounds well in the Lodge.

One highly objectionable form of words in the
closing may here be mentioned, in which the Worshipful Master issues his command to the Senior
Warden to 'close the Lodge *finally*,' and the Senior
Warden declares 'the Lodge *finally* closed....' If the
Lodge were never to be re-opened this form of words
would be quite appropriate, whereas the Junior
Warden follows immediately with the announcement
of the date of the next meeting.

In this very announcement by the Junior Warden,
the following words are often used : ' I declare this
meeting *adjourned* until,' etc. This is a mistake. If
the Lodge had to be adjourned, it would not be pre-

viously closed; there is no adjournment in any sense of the word. The Lodge is closed, and the Junior Warden should use this form :

J. W.—'And it is closed accordingly until (*state usual day*) in the ensuing month, except in case of emergency, of which due notice will be given.'

Then the Past Master closes the Volume of the Sacred Law, takes a step forward, or resumes his place on the daïs, and says :

'Brethren, nothing now remains but, according to ancient custom, that each Brother lock up the s...s of the Lodge in the safe and sacred repository, the heart, uniting in the act of F...y, F...y, F...y, and may God be with us all. So mote it be.'

The word F......y thrice repeated, the short invocation, and S. M. I. B., are set to music, and are included in the 'Lodge and Chapter Music' before mentioned. In singing the words, F......y, F......y, F..... y, the action is suited to each word as it would be if they were spoken. The practice of singing this concluding portion of the day's work is highly to be commended ; it rounds off, so to speak, and gives a solemn and impressive ending to the proceedings.

In certain cases it may be expedient, and even necessary, to close the Lodge summarily, by authority. The Rituals contain no instructions upon this subject. The following is a brief but sufficient form of closing :

W. M.—(Rises and gives one K....k, which is answered by the Wardens.) 'Brethren, by the authority with which I am invested, I close this Master Masons' Lodge.'

(Gives the K......s of the Second Degree, which are

then given by the Wardens, the Inner Guard, and the Tyler.)

In closing from the Second to the First Degree, the form is the same, only substituting the words, ' ... this Fellow-Crafts' Lodge.' There is no need to add, as is sometimes done, ' ... and the Lodge is now open in the Second Degree ' or ' ... is now open in the First Degree.' The several K......s after the declaration will have shown this, and furthermore, when the Lodge is closed in the Third Degree, whether in the regular form or by authority, it becomes *ipso facto* a Fellow-Crafts' Lodge, and when it is closed in the Second Degree, it becomes of necessity a Lodge in the First Degree, *without a verbal declaration to that effect in either case.*

In substantiation of this assertion it is only necessary to state that as the Lodge is opened first in the Entered Apprentice Degree, then in the Fellow-Crafts', and thirdly in the Master Masons' Degree, so it can be closed only by the reverse process in the same regular successive gradations. The Lodge cannot be opened directly, and at a bound, into the Second, or the Third Degree, so neither can it be closed at one swoop from either of those Degrees.

The ultimate closing should never be done in the summary form, but always in the regular way, ending with the prayer, etc., whether it be a regular meeting or a Lodge of emergency.

The form of calling the Lodge from labour to refreshment, and from refreshment to labour, is the same in the various Rituals, and it differs little in practice, except in so far as it is more or less (too often less) correctly rendered in the Lodge. The one only objection to which it lies open, as it stands in the Rituals, is, the use of the phrase ' high *time* ' in both calling off and recalling. There is extreme probability, amounting almost to a certainty, that *High Noon* is the old form, and the correct form. It precisely follows the meaning of the answer of the J. W. on defining his duty, namely, ' To mark the sun at its *meridian*, to call the Brethren from labour to refreshment,' etc. In the address at the investiture of the Junior Warden these words are used : ' I place you in your chair, which is situated in the South, the position in which you are enabled to mark the sun at its meridian, denoting " *High Noon*," the time for calling the Brethren from labour to refreshment at the Worshipful Master's command.' ' High Twelve ' is sometimes used, but we have twelve at midnight as well as twelve at noon. The words in common use, ' High Time ' and ' Past High Time,' are in-definite, if not unmeaning. ' High Noon ' is definite and clear, and is in strict accordance with the answer of the Junior Warden in the opening of the Lodge as previously quoted.

The intimate connection of the term, ' the sun at its meridian,' with the calling of ' the Brethren from labour to refreshment,' points unmistakably to High Noon as the time for refreshment ; and when the Junior Warden is asked the time, he should give the straightforward positive answer, ' High Noon, Worshipful Master,' and in calling from refreshment to labour, ' Past High Noon, Worshipful Master.'

Once upon a time—meaning of course a long time

ago—a certain Junior Warden, in calling the Lodge from labour to refreshment, instructed the brethren ' to keep within *'ail.'* One of the brethren remarked (*sotto voce*), 'Oh! we are to keep within *'ail;* I'll soon have some *ale* within me.' Atrocious, of course; doubly so, a bad pun upon bad grammar. Moral: take 'a firm and lionlike grip' of your ' h,' if not, he may slip out of his proper place, and then he may probably avenge the wrong, by forcing himself in where he has no right to be, as for example: the Junior Warden here quoted, during the opening in the Second Degree, when asked, 'Brother Junior Warden, are you a Fellow-Craft Freemason?' answered with especial emphasis, ' I *h*am, Worshipful Master, try me and prove me.' (See Appendix F, p. 246.)

This is no invention, no flight of fancy; it is 'an o'er true tale,' strictly and literally true, every word. Surely a flagrant breach of etiquette in emphasis.

CHAPTER XIII.

RETROSPECTIVE, AND AS TO NUMBER OF CANDIDATES AT ONE TIME.

Author may have laid himself open to Criticism—Questions appearing to belong rather to Ritual than to Etiquette—Limits and Boundaries difficult to define—Original Definition—The Guiding Principle—To Know the Reason Why—Opinions differ as to whether more than one Candidate may be taken at a time—No Law on the Subject—But Number must not exceed Five—All depends upon the Ability of the Officers—Privileges of a Lewis—A Wrong Idea—How to handle Several Candidates at one time—A Weariness of the Flesh—Perseverance thrown away—The Perambulations.

BEFORE commencing the consideration of the Ceremonies in the three Degrees, the author of this treatise feels called upon to acknowledge that he has to some extent laid himself open to criticism, in having somewhat freely gone into questions which would appear to belong rather to Ritual than to Etiquette. The truth is, it is extremely difficult to define the limits and boundaries of each; they so intermix and overlap, here and there, that it is next to impossible to say where the domain of the one ends and that of the other begins. On the one hand, one is bound to point out errors and defects in practice and procedure; and on the other, to suggest improvements, and to point out the better way, and in this way words, and forms of words, must be included, as well as gesture, position and demeanour.

Reverting to the definition of etiquette on page 15, we may see that it cannot be restricted—so far as we are concerned—to 'Regulations as to dress, demeanour, etc.'; but that we must take it in its wider acceptation of 'forms which are observed in particular places;' and this we may define as not only forms and modes of action, but also forms and modes of speech; and if, as we have shown in a previous chapter, it is true Etiquette to do the right thing, in the right way, at the right time, and in the right place, then it is equally Etiquette to say the right thing in the right way, at the right time and place.

This principle, applied to our Ritual, would lead us, while retaining as far as possible the forms of certain sentences, to add or to alter certain words, in order to render the meaning more clear, and the diction as a whole more harmonious, more dignified, and more worthy of 'our ancient and honourable Fraternity.'

This intention has been steadily kept in view in the preceding chapters; it will be the guiding principle in those which are to follow. The author trusts that, after this explanation of his ideas and motives, the reader will not cavil or complain, if here and there he finds some disquisitions upon the words of the Ritual, as well as upon subjects relating to action and demeanour, to position and procedure.

Therefore, when necessity compels, or it may appear to be expedient, some portions of the Ceremonies will be introduced, either in the exact words of the Ritual, or by a free description of the portion under discussion ; otherwise it would not be possible for the reader to understand the time when, and the place where, certain acts are required to be done, or certain positions are to be taken up, or certain forms of words are to be used. Thus elucidated, it is hoped that the recommendations contained in this volume will be found useful to many, more especially to the younger members of the craft who are, or who may in the future become, aspirants for Office in the Lodge.

The superstructure of eventual excellence in working can be raised only upon a foundation of sound knowledge, both theoretical and practical. For this reason, details apparently small and trivial, but, nevertheless, subserving some useful end, should not be overlooked. Every detail, small or great, is more readily committed to memory, and is better carried out in practice, if one knows the *reason why*, as regards time, place and manner of performance. *Experto crede.*

Opinions differ as to the number of Candidates upon whom either of the Ceremonies should be performed at one time ; that is, supposing there be more than one Candidate, shall they be taken together, or one at a time ? There is no law upon the subject. Rule 192 in the ' Book of Constitutions ' states that ' not more than five persons shall be initiated on the same day'; nothing more. The advocates of the custom of performing each Ceremony separately, upon each Candidate—say, up to and including the Obligation, and (in the Initiation) the restoration to L..., maintain that the Ceremony is more impressive with one only, than with two or three together, and that with more than one, some confusion is certain to occur. There is slight, if any, foundation for these objections. All must depend upon the manner in which the Worshipful Master, the Wardens, and more especially the Deacons, perform their several duties; the impressiveness depends in a great measure upon the Master; the orderliness and the avoidance of confusion and muddle depend upon the other officers.

Plenty of cases, frequently recurring, are within the experience of most of us, in which two or three Candidates taken at one time are initiated, passed, and raised, as efficiently and with as much impressiveness as could have been the case if the men had been taken seriatim. Many years ago the writer assisted at the Initiation (in the Apollo Lodge, Oxford) of five Candidates, all taken together. The Ceremony was performed with tolerable success; but the experiment is not to be commended, except under very extraordinary circumstances, and then only when all the Officers concerned are adepts in their several duties.

One of the five candidates was a Lewis, and he was allowed the 'privilege' to which he was entitled, namely, that of being made a Freemason *in precedence* of his fellow Candidates. Thus, his name stood first upon the Circular, and was the first mentioned at the door of the Lodge, and he was the foremost in the perambulation.

The privilege of a Lewis has this extent—no more.

8

A few years ago, on the occasion of the Initiation of one of the sons of H.R.H. the Grand Master, a short account of the event was given in one of the London daily papers. The writer of that description, evidently a Freemason, added: 'The young prince had not availed himself of the privilege which, as a Lewis (*i.e.*, the eldest son of a Freemason), he might have claimed, that of being made a Freemason before he had attained the full age of twenty-one years.'

This is a wrong idea altogether: no Lewis, be he Prince or peasant, can successfully claim such a privilege. Rule 186 in the Book of Constitutions is clear and emphatic upon the subject. Only by dispensation can any person be made a Freemason under the age of twenty-one years. The whole extent of the 'privilege' of a Lewis is, that it gives him precedence at his Initiation 'over any other person, however dignified by rank or fortune.'

We have shown that it is perfectly in accordance with the Constitutions, and with ordinary usage, to Initiate, Pass, or Raise more than one Candidate at one time; two or three are easily managed, but it is not desirable to go beyond three. In the case of four, or five, it is better to take them two and two, or three and two, up to and including the Obligation, and (in the Initiation) the restoration; and when the second detachment has reached the same stage, to take all together on to the end.

The writer was once present in a Lodge, in a large Provincial Town, when four Candidates were initiated on the same day; they were men of good social position in the locality, and an old Past Master of the Lodge had been asked to perform the Ceremony. He insisted upon taking the Candidates one at a time. Three perambulations were gone through with each man; during the first circuit he was taken to the Junior Warden, during the second to the Senior Warden, and then the brethren were told to 'take notice,' etc., and a third circuit of the Lodge was made. Then the Ceremony was gone through, up to and including the address upon Charity with each Candidate; a weariness of the flesh to all concerned, except to the old Past Master who performed the Ceremony, and who—in horsey parlance—never turned a hair, and literally revelled in the, to all but hismelf, intolerably tedious repetition.

One other instance may be cited. In another Lodge two Initiations, one Passing, and three Raisings, were performed on the same day, and each Candidate was taken through alone in each of the Degrees. Let us imagine the Third Degree performed up to and inclusive of 'that last and greatest trial,' and repeated three several times. Tedium inexpressible. The business commenced at 3 o'clock, and continued— with a short call-off for refreshment—until something past eight. Perseverance worthy of a better cause.

Above, on this page, it was mentioned that each of the four Candidates for Initiation was made to perform three perambulations. All the Rituals show clearly that there is a fixed and definite number of circuits to be performed in each Degree; namely, *one* for the First, *two* for the Second, and *three* for the Third Degree. We shall show, each in its own place, the reason, and the intention of the perambulations in each Degree; and we shall prove that in each case more than the prescribed number of perambulations would be superfluous, and less than the several numbers would be insufficient.. No Master of a Lodge is justified in causing, or allowing the Candidate in either degree to perform more than the established number of perambulations; the rule is clear, and, in accordance with reason, it should be held to be a *Landmark in Freemasonry.*

CHAPTER XIV.

INITIATION OF A CANDIDATE.

In the remarks which we may have to make upon the three Ceremonies, the word 'Candidate' will be used, for the sake of brevity and convenience; but this may always be understood to mean 'Candidate or Candidates,' and not as at all implying a preference for taking them singly through each Ceremony. The writer was Initiated, Passed, and Raised, in company with two others (his memory is very clear upon the point), and there was no hitch or want of impressiveness in any of those Ceremonies. He has himself performed the Ceremonies numberless times upon two and three Candidates at the same time, and he has in no case experienced the slightest difficulty, nor, he believes, has the Ceremony lost anything in seriousness or impressiveness in consequence.

The preparation of a Candidate for the Ceremony of Initiation has been mentioned in an earlier Chapter, and the reader was referred to Appendix E, page 242, for a full explanation of the *origin* and the *intention* of every detail of that preparation. The theory and practice of the several K......s, namely, those constituting a report in each Degree, and those constituting an alarm in each Degree, are fully detailed, and explained on page 74.

We will suppose the Candidate to have been properly prepared, the *alarm* (one K....k) to have been sounded, the Candidate admitted, the Prayer recited, and after the question : ' In whom do you put your trust ?' he is instructed by the Junior Deacon to reply ' In God.' It will be noticed that the Name by which the Almighty is generally known to the outer world is here given, as it is also in the Worshipful Master's rejoinder, ' Right glad am I,' etc. The reason why that Name is used in this place, and not the more ample title T. G. A. O. T. U., is probably because the shorter name is familiar to the Candidate, and would have more force than would the longer and unfamiliar title. The full title is used in the beginning of the Obligation, but the more familiar name is used in the last clause, which contains the attestation in common use in Courts of Justice and elsewhere ; the words being identical, therefore familiar to the Candidate, and more likely to act forcibly upon his mind, and to remain in his memory. These cases are those mentioned on page 103 as being exceptions to the rule there laid down upon the subject.

It is generally the custom for both the Deacons to receive the Candidate at the door ; but the Junior Deacon has him in his especial charge after the conclusion of the Prayer. He should be from the commencement always on the alert to suggest the proper answers to the questions asked by the Worshipful Master from time to time. The two Deacons cross their wands over the Candidate during the Prayer ; when that is concluded the Senior Deacon resumes his seat, except there be more than one Candidate ; in that case he would, as a matter of course, take charge of one of them ; but the Junior Deacon would lead throughout the Ceremony.

One sometimes hears in the Lodge—and it stands thus in some existing Rituals—' *Right ;* glad am I,' etc. This is a misconception. The correct reading is the old form, ' Right glad am I.' Many similar expressions are still in partial use, *e.g.*, ' Right merrily ;' ' Right heartily ;' and in the old song, ' …hath won my right goodwill ' (' The Lass of Richmond Hill ').

An objectionable form of words is found in some Rituals, and as a consequence is often heard in the Lodge, ' …and follow your leader.' This is too suggestive of the boys' game, ' Follow my leader.' Besides, the Candidate does not follow ; the Junior Deacon takes his *right* hand in his own *left*, and they walk *side* by *side*.

The better form of words is, ' …you may safely arise and *accompany* your *guide*,' etc.

A question may here be discussed, namely, should the Worshipful Master in calling the attention of the brethren to the preparation of the Candidate, say, 'The brethren *from* the North, East, South, and West,' or '*in* the North, East,' etc.? The brethren of each Lodge are usually resident, or have their occupation in the locality in which the Lodge is held; but even in the event of their being gathered from the four winds, that would not affect the question at issue. The course of the Candidate is clearly defined in the Second Section of the First Lecture, '...he (the Junior Deacon) took me by the right hand, and led me up the North, past the Worshipful Master in the East, down the South, and finally delivered me over to the Senior Warden in the West.'

The Worshipful Master's command to the Brethren, being identical (in so far as the cardinal points of the compass are concerned) with this description of the course of the Candidate, would seem to show that the situation of the Brethren *in* the Lodge at the time is intended, and not the point of the compass in which the residence of each may be situated; it can be of little consequence where he hails *from*, it is simply a question of the place *in* the Lodge which he occupies at that moment, be it *in* the North, *in* the East, *in* the South, or *in* the West.

In an ordinary way, if one were asked to name the cardinal points of the compass, he would say, North, South, East, and West, whereas here we have them placed in the exact order in which the course of the Candidate lies, consequently he would first be brought under the observation of the Brethren seated in the North, and thence severally of those seated in the East, the South, and the West, and the fact that the

Brethren seated *in* those several portions of the Lodge are called upon in that same order of sequence, would seem to be conclusive proof of our contention, namely, that the then position of the Brethren is the point at issue, and not the situation relatively to the Lodge of their several residences.

The attention of the Brethren having been called to the fact that the Candidate is about to pass in view before them, he is conducted up the North, across the East end of the Lodge— the Deacon saluting as he passes the Master—down the South, and is halted on the right of the Junior Warden. We will here explain the theory of the one perambulation of the Lodge in the First Degree. It is this : The Candidate has to pass through *three* doorways, one real, two imaginary, and at each of these the same alarm is sounded, and the same examination by question and answer is made ; that is, all that transpires at the actual door of the Lodge is repeated in act and in word in the examination by the two Wardens, who severally are the guardians of the two imaginary doors.

This theory of the three doors is no fanciful idea ; upon no other hypothesis can we account for the exact repetition, three several times, of the one K....k (the alarm) and of the questions and answers, and especially for the fact that the Candidate is bidden by each of the Wardens to 'Enter free.'* If these words 'Enter free ' do not signify the permission of

* These words may probably mean ' Enter freely.' In some lodges, however, a different meaning is given to them, thus : ' Enter free and of good report.' This form has much to recom· mend it, following closely as it does the words of the last answer in the examination.

the guardian of a portal or entrance of some kind for the Candidate to enter that—be it what it may—of which the Warden has the guardianship, then the word *enter* is an absurdity.

The following explanation of what is done at each Warden's chair will make this clear.   The Candidate stands on the right of the Junior Warden; he—the Junior Warden—is, for the time being, supposed to be guarding a door, representing the door which, the Volume of the Sacred Law informs us, 'was in the right side of the house' (1 Kings vi. 8), at the foot of the Winding Staircase which led to the Middle Chamber of King Solomon's Temple, and which, as our traditions inform us, was guarded by the Ancient Junior Warden.   Here—one K....k—corresponding with the K....k on the entrance-door (*the alarm*) is given with the right hand of the Candidate guided by the Junior Deacon, upon the extended right arm of the Junior Warden; the arm representing the door, the one K....k being an alarm; the questions are asked and answered as at the entrance of the Lodge, and the Candidate receives permission to pass this imaginary door, in the words, 'Enter free.'   He is then conducted to the Senior Warden, who is supposed to be guarding a door, representing the door which stood at the top of the Winding Staircase, and which was guarded by the ancient Senior Warden. The *one* K....k is given upon the right arm of the Senior Warden, the questions are asked and answered as before, and the Candidate receives permission to pass this imaginary door also, in the words, 'Enter free.'   He is then presented to the Worshipful Master by the Senior Warden, 'a Candidate properly prepared to be made a Freemason.'

From this explanation it will be seen that the one perambulation is indispensably necessary, firstly, in order that the brethren may see that the Candidate is properly prepared, and secondly, that he may be made to pass through the two imaginary doorways, sounding the alarm upon each, and being verbally examined as to his qualifications separately by the two Wardens, the several guardians of the two supposititious doors.

It will be clear, also, that more than one perambulation is not only unnecessary, but would involve the irregularity of the Candidate *passing by* (without the regular formalities) the two doors, instead of *entering freely through* the doorways, according to 'the immemorial custom and tradition of the Craft' in this First Degree.

During the questions which follow the presentation, the Junior Deacon should be ready to suggest the proper reply to each, namely, 'I do,' 'I do,' and 'I will.' It is better to prompt the replies than to leave them to the Candidate, whose form of words in reply may perhaps be not well chosen.

'The method of advancing from West to East in this degree' is unfortunately often not well understood by the Deacons themselves. The S...s are wrongly dictated. The position of the feet should be h... to h..., *in the form of a Square ;* the Deacon too often instructs the Candidate to place the r... h... in the h... of the l... f..., *thus forming a Level.* The latter is the position by which the Candidate is instructed to advance towards the Worshipful Master at a later stage of the Ceremony, and he is then informed that ' This is the first R... S... in Freemasonry,' showing that the S...s, in advancing from West to East, are, and should always be, separate and distinct from that first ' R...... S....'   The confusion of these S...s, the one form with the other, is inexcusably frequent ; it cannot be too strongly reprobated.

CHAPTER XV.

INITIATION OF A CANDIDATE (CONTINUED).

'Masonry is Free'—Posture during the O. B.—It cannot be
done as directed—What the J. D. should do—Deacon should
be ready to prompt during the O. B.—The Action of the
W. M.—The word 'hele'—The Invocation—'A Serious
Promise,' forsooth !—A Matter for great Care on the Deacon's
Part—Musical Service comes in well here—Candidate not yet
a *Brother*, only a *Novice*—W. M. will find it more convenient
to leave the Chair here—How the Examination should proceed—When the Candidate is asked for a Charitable Contri-
bution—Explanation of the Working Tools—A System that
works well—Not Operative Masons—The By-Laws—The
Salute on leaving the Lodge—S. or J. W. may deliver the
Charge—Some old and ridiculous Customs.

WE may venture to suggest that the words in the
earlier portion of the Master's address to the Candidate previously to the Obligation, namely, 'Masonry
is free,' is abrupt, and to the uninitiated man not
clearly intelligible. He will have been so accustomed
to associate *masonry* with the building trade that the
meaning of the words quoted would never occur to him.
A better form, and one incapable of misconstruction, is
' ...... to inform you that the Speculative Masonry
which we practise is *essentially* free....'

The instruction given to the Candidate as to his
posture during the Obligation contains these words,
'... place your r... f... in the form of a square,' a
clear impossibility; one f... alone cannot form a

square, it can only form one arm of it in conjunction
with another f..., and in this case the Candidate's
other f... is otherwise disposed of. It is better to say,
' placing your r... f... at right angles with the body.'
There is always a great deal of pulling and pushing,
in order to get the position indicated. No one, except
a man who is what is commonly called splay-footed,
can, while *squarely breasting* the Pedestal, and having
both hands engaged, and k...g on the l...k, place the
r... f... perfectly at right angles with the body. The
Junior Deacon should place the Candidate's r... f...
well forward, say about the centre of the right side of
the kneeling-stool, do the best he can as to the angle,
study the balance of the body in an easy position, and
accept that position as a sufficient fulfilment of the
requirement of the case. Great discomfort—at times
amounting to physical pain—must frequently be the
result of the Deacon's ill-directed energy in the way
indicated.

During the Obligation the Deacon should be ready
to suggest the right word, or sentence, if—as frequently
happens—the Candidate fails to catch, or he misunder-
stands, or fails to repeat correctly, the words dictated
by the Worshipful Master ; in either of these cases
the Deacon should correct the mistake, and save the
Master the trouble of repeating the words himself.

In some Lodges the Worshipful Master says, ' substituting your name for mine.' This, as everyone's
experience will show, is productive of a bungle in the
great majority of cases. The Candidate almost invariably repeats the name of the Worshipful Master as
given to him, and he has to be set right. No good

reason can be given for the retention of the custom. It is almost as reprehensible as practical joking to set a trap into which the unwary is almost certain to fall ; it is not etiquette, and there is no reason why it should be done.

When the words ' hereby and hereon ' are spoken, the Worshipful Master should place his hand lightly —for a moment—upon the hand of the Candidate, otherwise the latter, being in a S... of d..., those words would be unintelligible. The word ' hele ' used in the Obligation is an old English word which signifies ' to hide or to cover or conceal.' It is derived from the ancient Saxon word ' helan,' from which we derive the word ' hell.'

The Obligation ends with the words, ' So help me, God, and may He keep me steadfast in this *the great* and *solemn obligation* of an Entered Apprentice Freemason,' and yet some of the Rituals make the Master to say, ' What you have repeated may be considered *but a serious promise.*' What, then, mean the words, ' so help me, God ' and ' the great and solemn obligation,' which the Master has just previously caused the Candidate to repeat ? It is a case of stultification, perfect and complete ; a solemn obligation which the Almighty is invoked to help the Candidate to keep, is ' but a serious promise !'

The words ' so help me, God,' are identical with those in use in all our courts of justice. Imagine the functionary who administers this oath in court, telling a witness that ' what he has repeated may be considered but a serious promise.' One would like to hear what some of our judges would have to say to that official. And yet our Obligation renders the words far more solemn than they sound in a court of Justice, by the words that precede them, that is 'without evasion, equivocation, or mental reservation,' and by those that follow, namely, '... and may He keep me steadfast,' and we may add also the solemn words at the beginning of the Obligation, 'I, A. B., in the presence of T. G. A. O. T. U.,' and those other words, '... hereby and hereon *most solemnly and sincerely swear ...*' A serious promise forsooth! What, then, constitutes a solemn oath?

The old compilers of the Rituals went upon the supposition that the kissing of the Book was the 'be all and end all' of an oath; consequently that the invocation of the Sacred Name stands for nothing in this matter, the truth being that the kissing of the Book is just a form of attestation of a man's belief in the Almighty, Whose Name he has just previously invoked, and Whose Eternal Existence, and Whose attributes of Omnipotence, Omniscience, and Omnipresence are revealed in the Sacred Volume, which he then salutes with his lips.

If the terms of the Obligation amounted *but to a serious promise*, the kissing of the Book alone could not convert it into '*a solemn obligation;*' but that act does testify that the Oath which he has solemnly sworn by the name of the God of the Bible is strictly binding upon his conscience.

It should be noted also, that neither this formula (about the serious promise), nor any form of words at all like it, is used in the Second or the Third Degree. If it be necessary in any one Degree, it is equally necessary in all; and conversely, if it be unnecessary in the two higher Degrees, it is equally unnecessary in the First Degree. It should be expunged from the Rituals, and its use should be discontinued in our Lodges. A great mistake was made when it was introduced, but, ''Tis never too late to mend.'

The restoration to l... requires very great care on the part of the Deacon—he has to be ready to suggest the proper word in reply to the Master's question, and at the same time to have all prepared for the denouement *at the proper moment.* It is well also for the whole of the Brethren to look to the East, so that the salute may be given by all *as by one man.* A volley, and not a dropping fire, should welcome the Candidate on his R...n to L...t. The effect of the whole may be, and often is, marred by want of proper attention to the details here mentioned.

Where the musical services, before mentioned, are in use, the restoration is preceded and led up to by a portion of an appropriate and suggestive verse; this, when sung, and of course concluded with the salute, has a fine effect. It is highly to be commended.

We shall scarcely be going beyond the legitimate scope of our subject if we notice the form of words, in frequent use, in bidding the Candidate to rise, namely: 'Rise, duly (some say *newly*) obligated *Brother*, among Freemasons.' The Candidate is not yet a Brother in the full sense, nor, we may say, in any sense of the word. We will take a possible instance : suppose that at this point, from sudden illness, or from any other cause, the Candidate were compelled to leave the Lodge (this has occurred in the writer's presence), would he be received into any Lodge as a 'Brother among Freemasons?' No; he has not been entrusted with the S..., the G... and the W...; he has not been invested, and he has not been tested by the appeal in the cause of Charity. One of the reasons given for this appeal applies to our argument, and strengthens it. It is this: '. . . that you had neither ...... nor ...... *of value* about you, for if you had, the Ceremony of your Initiation thus far must have been repeated,' so that even at this late stage of the Ceremony the Candidate, so far from being a fully qualified *brother*, would be liable to have to go through the Ceremony again, if one important part of his preparation had been omitted.

As it is true etiquette to give to every man the appellation of the rank to which he is justly entitled, so it would show ignorance or carelessness, which is a breach of etiquette, to give him a title higher than that which he by right possesses. The Candidate at the time now in question is *in statu pupillari*, in his *novitiate*, in fact; therefore, a correct form of words would be, 'Rise, duly obligated *novice*, in the First Degree in Freemasonry.'

The idea of the use of the word 'novice,' to designate a Candidate whose Initiation is not completed, is not new. A Ritual which was in general use fifty years ago (in the direction which the Worshipful Master gives to the Deacon after the investiture), has these words: '. . . you will now place the *noviciate* (*sic*) in the N. E. C.,' etc. The word *novice* was here intended, and it is clear that the Candidate was considered to be in a probationary condition up to and during the address upon Charity and the appeal to the novice ; so it is premature to hail him as a ' Brother among Freemasons ' immediately after the Obligation.

After directing attention to the three lesser lights, it will be found to be more convenient for the Worshipful Master to descend from the daïs, and to face the Candidate (who remains in the N.E., facing south). If, as is sometimes done, the Master attempts to communicate the S... without leaving his place, he has several difficulties to contend with : the pedestal and the candlestick prevent him from easily and clearly showing the S...p and the f...t in the form of a S...e ; there is a difficulty in taking the Candidate's hand, the candlestick being in the way—in fact, he has to manœuvre a good deal during the process, whereas by descending to the floor it is all plain sailing. The Master must of necessity leave his chair—and during a considerable period—in the Third Degree ; no valid reason can be given against his leaving it for a short time in the First and the Second Degrees.

When the Novice is conducted to the J. W., the examination should proceed as far as the W..., and should not include the derivation and the interpretation, etc. These, however, should always be given to the S. W. in full. It should be clearly understood that the import of the W... is *not* S..., but *in* S....

After the address upon Charity the Deacon should suggest the reply, not leaving the form of words to the choice of the Novice ; he can then truthfully repeat the reply to the Worshipful Master. During the short address following this reply, a very distinguished

Master of the Apollo (University) Lodge in Oxford used to interpolate the following words. After the words, 'sport with your feelings,' he added, '*or to raise a laugh at your expense.*' He had from time to time noticed among the younger members of the Lodge a tendency to make merry over the non-plussed look of the Novice at the time of the salver being presented to him. This would never have occurred if the Deacon had performed his duty with the necessary tact and readiness, and perhaps we may add seriousness.

The author of this work was present and assisted at the Initiation of M. Jullien (the originator of the Popular Promenade Concerts in London), in the Apollo Lodge in Oxford. When the appeal in the cause of Charity was made to him, before the reply could be suggested, he, with true French vivacity, said: 'I have . . . . but I *will give you a cheque.*'

In many exceedingly well-worked Lodges the Worshipful Master and the Senior and the Junior Warden each takes a part in the explanation of the Working Tools, the Master having the Twenty-four inch Gauge, the Senior Warden the Gavel, and the Junior Warden the Chisel. The newly-initiated brother is placed on the North side of the Lodge facing the Junior Warden, and he is thus enabled to see each speaker in turn. If this be well done by the three Principal Officers, the explanation comes with a more impressive effect than it does usually from the Master alone, whose sole voice with little interval will have been heard throughout the Cere-mony. This opinion is given not as a mere speculation, but as the result of observation and of *personal experience. The system works well in the Lodge.*

Between that portion of the explanation which describes the use of the Working Tools in Operative Masonry, and the following part which applies them in a moral sense, one often hears the words, ' but as we are not *all Operative.*' This is a mistake. In the Lodge we are *all* purely *Speculative* Masons ; we neither practise nor profess ' Operative Masonry'; and if any men who are really masons by trade become members of the Order, they leave their business behind when they enter the Lodge, and are for the time being as completely Speculative Masons as are other members whose business or occupation is of a different character. A better form of words (better because they are in strict accordance with fact) is this : W. M.—' But we, *not professing* to be Operative, but Free and Accepted,' etc. This is clear, straightforward, and literally true.

Mention is made in Chapter V., page 50, of the custom in certain Lodges of actually presenting a copy of the Book of Constitutions, and one of the By-laws, to every Entered Apprentice. Good reasons are there given for this practice, and to these the reader will do well to refer.

Previously to being conducted out of the Lodge, the newly-initiated brother is told that on his return a Charge will be delivered, and the older Rituals add the words, 'also an Explanation of the Tracing Board, if time will permit.' This would be quite right if the Tracing Board were intended to be explained, but this rarely happens. Unfortunately

Masters are by no means rare who repeat these words, parrot-like, at every Initiation, making in effect a promise which there is no intention to perform.

Before leaving the Lodge, the Deacon instructs his charge to salute the Worshipful Master, and he should, if necessary, correct any informality or slovenliness in the performance of the salute. A mere raising the hand to the appointed position should not be allowed; the hand should be thrown out boldly to the front, and then with a free circular sweep of the arm the hand is brought into the desired position, not placed at once . . . . but first to one side, and then drawn into position, with the hand not bent, but forming a line with the forearm, the elbow being well raised, not drooping. This position, and the manner of assuming it, should be uniformly practised by every member when entering or leaving the Lodge, or when commanded to stand to order. A perfunctory or slovenly manner of giving the salute is a breach of Masonic etiquette. It is a simple and graceful act of courtesy on the part of the Worshipful Master to acknowledge the salutation by a corresponding salute in return.

It is a by no means rare occurrence to hear the Senior or the Junior Warden deliver the Charge in this Degree. This is a relief to the Master, and an advantage to the Wardens, as being good practice in anticipation of their higher duties in the future. For some remarks upon the Charge see Appendix G, page 249.

Some personal recollections of old and highly objectionable practices during the Initiation may

here be given. During the obligation, when the P...
of the O... is stated in words, the writer has seen a
Past Master take up the twenty-four inch gauge, and
figuratively perform the act upon the Candidate, to
his great surprise, if not alarm. He has also seen
during the Prayer a large cavalry sword held to the
breast of the Candidate, and at the moment when he
avows his trust in God, the sword is dropped to the
floor with a great clatter, a practical exposition perfectly unintelligible to the Candidate in his then
condition, as was that of the figurative action in the
Obligation, both, therefore, perfectly useless and consequently superfluous, besides being highly objectionable as tending to disturb the equanimity of the
Candidate. An old custom—let us hope no longer
permitted — was in existence within the writer's
memory. During the perambulation, when the Candidate was passing the fireplace, the fire-irons were
rattled, or the poker ostentatiously thrust into the
fire—a proceeding utterly unworthy of our Order, and
one of which those who practised it should have been
heartily ashamed.

Another custom—not as mischievous, but still very
objectionable—is still practised in some few Lodges.
When, in perambulating the Lodge, the Candidate
approaches the Junior Warden's chair, he (the J. W.)
instead of *receiving* the ' Alarm,' gives a loud sounding
knock upon his pedestal, startling to a strong man,
alarming to a weak one. On approaching the Senior
Warden, the same thing is repeated. Comment is
unnecessary.

CHAPTER XVI.

THE SECOND DEGREE

WE stated in a former chapter, page 76, *q.v.*, that when a Candidate for the Second Degree is conducted to the door of the Lodge, the K...s of the First Degree should be given as constituting *an alarm*, and the reasons were fully explained why those K...s, and no others, should be given. We stated also on page 115 that the number of perambulations in the Second Degree was two. We will now show, by that which has to be done in each round, that less than two circuits would be insufficient, and that more are unnecessary, and a waste of time.

During the first perambulation the Candidate has to prove to the Brethren that he has been duly initiated, and for this purpose he is conducted to the Junior Warden, who subjects him to an examination,

in which he is called upon to communicate the S...,
the S..., the G..., and the W..., which had been communicated to him at his Initiation. After passing the
Senior Warden's pedestal, and having thus made one
circuit, the Brethren are bidden to observe that he
'is about to pass in view before them, to show that
he is properly prepared,' etc. In the second round
he has to prove to the Senior Warden that he is in
possession of the P... G... and P... W..., leading
from the First to the Second Degree. Each perambulation, therefore, has its purpose and its object, and
when the two rounds have been completed nothing
more in the way of examination has to be done, and
the Candidate is presented as being properly prepared
to be passed to the Second Degree.

A difference in practice will be found in different
Lodges, as to the manner of the examination by the
Junior Warden, during the first circuit. In many,
probably the majority of Lodges, the Junior Warden
instructs the Candidate to give ' the W... freely, and
in full.' In others he is required to l... or h... it.
The first and more general system saves time ; the
second has the merit of keeping alive in the Candidate's memory the counsel of prudence inculcated at
his Initiation.

After the second perambulation, on reaching the
West, the Candidate is called upon to communicate
to the Senior Warden the P... G... and the P... W....
When asked for ' the import of that w...' he is taught
to answer P...y. This is not the meaning of the W...,
it is literally ' an ear of corn ' in some sentences in
the Bible, and ' a flowing stream ' in others.

The word S... has this double meaning, and is therefore correctly depicted in the Tracing Board. The *word* does not mean 'P...y,' but its double signification may, when united, be said to symbolize 'P...y.' Eminent Hebrew scholars have been consulted as to the interpretation of the word, and there exists no difference of opinion between them, except that one rather favours the 'stream of water,' inasmuch as the word was used as a *T*... *beside a stream.* Nevertheless, a multitude of texts have been quoted in which the word is used in such connections that no other meaning *in those places* can be assigned to it than 'an Ear of Corn;' but no case can be cited in which the word alone can by any means be rendered 'P ..y.'

A change of a very few words in the questions and answers will bring in the correct meaning of the word, and still retain the word P...y as follows :

S. W.—To this P... G... a W... is attached, which I will thank you for.

CAN.—S....

S. W.—What does this W... imply ?

CAN.—An Ear of Corn or a Stream of Water.

S. W.—How is it depicted in a Fellow-Crafts' Lodge ?

CAN.—By an Ear of Corn near a Stream of Water.

S. W.—What is the import of *that symbol ?*

CAN.—P...y.

S. W.—Pass, ...

The method of advancing from West to East having been verbally explained, the Candidate should be placed on the North side of the Lodge, about six feet to the West of the Master's pedestal, and facing full South ; then, by describing 'a fourth part of a circle,' the 'proper steps' will bring him to the proper place.

Some of the remarks made upon the Obligation in the First Degree apply with equal force to the one in the Second, and the reader would do well to refer to pages 126-7 inclusive. A mistake is often made in placing the l... h... in the proper position ; it should rest in the angle of the S..., and not the elbow on the S... with the l... h... elevated. That position of the l... h... comes in a later stage of the proceedings.

At the conclusion of the Obligation the Worshipful Master is made to say, 'Rise, duly obligated Fellow-Craft Freemason.' The argument against a similar form of words in the First Degree applies with equal force here (see page 129). The Candidate is not yet a Fellow-Craft, but he is something less of a *Novice* in Freemasonry than he was in the corresponding stage of his Initiation ; he is *on probation*, therefore the words, 'Rise, Probationer in the Second Degree,' apply perfectly to his case.

In imparting the S..., the Worshipful Master, assisted by the Senior Deacon, should see that the Candidate makes each portion of the three forms accurately, fairly, and squarely, especially in the H... S..., in which, not only is the arm placed at 'an angle of ninety Degrees,' but the th... is also, and is clearly pointed over the l... s..., and not as a visitor to various Lodges in some Northern Provinces too often sees, stretched out *across*, with the *palm of the hand forward.* An opinion upon this point has been obtained from high authority, and the custom here condemned has been pronounced to be entirely wrong. This portion of the three-fold S..., made in the proper form, is an appropriate posture of Invocation, whereas, when made in the wrong way as described, it is a *repellant gesture*, and is altogether contrary to the sense of the words which accompany it.

A great difference of opinion exists as to the locality in which these words were uttered, as well as in the rendering of the words themselves. The older Rituals lay the scene of the battle in the Valley of Jehoshaphat, a very extraordinary and entirely unfounded supposition. Newer versions of the Ritual favour the Valley of Rephidim, but then they have to omit all mention of the sun standing still; this event has always been connected with the H... S..., and its omission deprives the S... of much of its meaning, and all its interest, and force. Instead of the older connection of Joshua, and the sun standing still, the newer copies bring in Moses, having his 'hands stayed up by Aaron and Hur, the one on the one side, and the other on the other side; and his hands were steady until the going down of the sun.' Here both hands are shown to have been held up, and *both certainly at the same elevation.* This does not at all apply to our H... S.... It is curious to notice that in the case of Moses he is said (in the newer Rituals) to have '*prayed fervently* to the Almighty for the overthrow of the Amalekites;' and in the case of Joshua (in the older Rituals), '. . . he *prayed fervently* that the Almighty would continue the light of day. . . .' The Bible says nothing of the kind. Moses had his hands held up, but there is no mention of his uttering a word. Joshua did not *pray*, fervently or otherwise; he *commanded* the sun to stand still.

'The effectual fervent prayer of a righteous man availeth much,' but we have no right to assert that prayer was offered, in any case in which the Bible is silent upon the subject, or in which, as in the case of Joshua, the text shows to the contrary.

An unprejudiced examination of the facts, which undoubtedly connect the miracle with Joshua, and both with a certain locality (see Joshua x. 11-13), must lead to the conclusion that our H... S... is derived from the events recorded in those verses; and we have no right to twist and pervert the text in order to bring in certain theories, which, upon examination, will be found to have no foundation in reason or in the Bible.

The elimination of the reference to the Sun in the newer Rituals may well be called the removal of an ancient Landmark, and certainly an 'innovation in the body of Freemasonry.'

A foot-note in one of the Rituals mentioned runs thus: 'The reference is generally made to Joshua x. 11-13, *but historically that is an error.*' Where is the error? The words are in the Bible, the detail of events is undeniable, the connection of the events with the S... clear to demonstration, and yet we are told—*without a word of argument or reason in proof*—that '*historically that is* an error!' A bold assertion to be made without an atom of evidence in its support.

The following rendering of the whole passage reconciles all difficulties as to the man, the place, and the words, the latter being, as they should be, the very words of the Bible:

'The second is given thus...　It is called the H... S... or S... of P....　This is said to have been the S... used by Joshua when fighting the battles of the Lord "in the going down to Beth-horon."　In this position he spake those memorable words, "Sun, stand thou still upon Gibeon: and thou, Moon, in the valley of Ajalon.　And the sun stood still, and the moon stayed, until the people had avenged themselves upon their enemies."'

(The foregoing is an excerpt from 'The Revised Ritual.')

A perversion of Scripture is a breach of etiquette of the worst description, and when the spurious sentence is inferior to the original in significance and force of expression it is altogether inexcusable.

One exception to this rule, however, seems to be forced upon us by ancient usage, and that is the passage quoted at the end of the communication of the S...s, etc., of this Degree; but it should never be given without some qualifying words, such as these: 'The former word denotes in S..., the latter to E..., and when conjoined they symbolize S...b...y, *for according to our traditions* God said in S... I will E... this My house that it may stand firm for ever.'　This passage is not to be found in the Bible.　The nearest to it is, 'He shall build me a house, and I will establish his throne for ever.'　This latter passage, however, does not contain the words which are required, in order to identify the quotation with the meaning which we assign to the names of the two Great Pillars.

The association of our interpretation of the meaning of the names with a passage which is supposed to be from Holy Writ, is of such ancient date and usage, it has become so engrafted into the form of communicating the S...s, that we cannot now eliminate it, if indeed we wished and endeavoured to do so ; and when it is explained that the words are 'according to our traditions,' and therefore not professing that they are the very words of the Bible, the use of them is not open to very serious objection. On the other hand, to use the words ' For God said,' etc., without explanation, is highly objectionable.

The 'Explanation of the Working Tools of the Second Degree' gives occasion to point out one of the greatest anomalies in the whole of the Ceremonies of the three Degrees. In most of the published Rituals the explanation of the Square, the Level, and the Plumb-rule is given with extreme brevity in the Ceremony of Passing to the *Second Degree*, whereas in the Explanation of the Tracing Board of *the First Degree* they—the Working Tools of the Second Degree—are explained at unusual length.

Very little consideration is needed to show how entirely wrong this is. The case stands thus. The Explanation of the First Tracing Board must of necessity be given when the Lodge is opened in the First, or Entered Apprentice Degree, and in it the Rituals—most of them—give the long Explanation of the Working Tools of the Second, or Fellow-Craft's,

Degree; and then in the Ceremony of Passing, *during which alone* the Working Tools of the Second Degree *can lawfully* be explained, they are slurred over with a brevity not to be found in the Explanation of the Working Tools of the First or of the Third Degree.

This utter *bouleversement* ought to be reversed; the lengthy explanation of the uses of these Tools in Operative Masonry, and of their moral signification, should be expunged from the First Tracing Board, and should be restored to the Ceremony of Passing, to which they legitimately belong.

The implements in question, being the 'Movable Jewels' of the Lodge, and being severally the distinctive badges of the Master and the two Wardens, must of necessity be mentioned in the Tracing Board of the First Degree, but not necessarily described and moralized upon; they should be mentioned only in the quality of Movable Jewels, and as designating the three Principal Officers of the Lodge; it is unconstitutional to explain them.

The description of their uses and the excellent moral lessons which they teach (the latter being far too good to be lost), should be transferred bodily from the Tracing Board to their proper place in the Second Ceremony. Without this longer exposition of the Working Tools, the Ceremony of Passing is poor and meagre as compared with the Initiation and the Raising; whereas with the full explanation it will compare not unfavourably with the First and the Third Ceremonies.

More than fifty years ago the author of this work performed the Ceremony of Passing (in Oxford) in the presence of a Past Grand Officer of high rank in Grand Lodge. He explained the Working Tools (as he always did and does still) at full length, and the distinguished visitor expressed his high approval of the *restoration* of that Explanation *to its proper place.*

In a recently published Ritual (to which allusion has previously been made) the very brief explanation of the Working Tools of this Degree is given ; a foot-note is added which runs thus :

' Sometimes a longer explanation of the symbolic teaching of the Working Tools is given as follows, but it is only adopted in the " Emulation " working in the course of the Lectures. (See *First* Lecture, Fifth Section.)'

The foot-note then gives the full explanation before-mentioned, for which see Appendix H, p. 254.

This question rises above the sphere of etiquette ; it is a question of right or wrong, of lawfulness or unlawfulness ; it comes clearly within the scope of ' the minor Jurisprudence of the Craft.' It is clearly contrary to the spirit of our Constitution to explain in a Lodge which is opened only in the First Degree, and in which Entered Apprentices may be present, the uses and the moral signification of the Working Tools of the Fellow-Craft's Degree, as much so as it would be to introduce into the Tracing Board of the Second Degree the Working Tools of a Master-Mason.

No sophistry can justify this serious infraction of constitutional right, no plea of customary usage can palliate it ; it is utterly wrong in principle, and it should not be permitted in practice.

In the fifth section of the First Lecture the Square, the Level, and the Plumb-rule are named as the Movable Jewels of the Lodge, and as the distinguishing emblems severally of the Worshipful Master and of the Senior and the Junior Wardens.   In the working of this section in the Lodge, each of these Principal Officers rises in his place, and holding up his special Jewel, explains the duty devolving upon him as the wearer of that Jewel.   These several explanations are good and sufficient, and are perfectly constitutional, inasmuch as they relate only to each implement as a *Jewel*, and not as a *Working Tool*.

The fact of the Worshipful Master and the two Wardens—when working the Fifth Section of the First Lecture—explaining, each for himself, the teaching of the Jewel by which he is officially distinguished, may be taken to establish a precedent, to be followed when the explanation of the same implements, in the character of Working Tools, is given in the Second Degree ; namely, that each of the three principal officers should rise in his place, holding in his hand the Implement by which he is officially distinguished, and explain in succession—the Master, the Square ; the Senior Warden, the Level; and the Junior Warden, the Plumb-rule.   This would be to adopt the custom mentioned on page 132 ; and with the longer explanation, the change of voice comes with refreshing effect.   That which may rightly and constitutionally be done in the Lectures may with equal constitutional right be done in the Ceremonies. Reason is on its side, and *there is no law against it.*

CHAPTER XVII.

THE THIRD DEGREE.

At the Door of the Lodge—The Three Perambulations—The Examination—What the Candidate has to Pass Over—The Third Tracing Board—An Inexpensive Substitute—An Undergraduate's Wit—Remarks on the O. B.—Not yet *M. M.*, still only a *Probationer*—Wardens had better Leave their Places now, and be ready to Change with the Deacons—Thus the Narrative will not be Disturbed—The Wardens should be specially Careful in Performing their respective Functions—The S. W. before the Final Action—Details of Position and Action require Care—Candidate now in the N.—Instructed how to Advance—A necessary Caution—An Absurd Effect—The Permission to Retire—Trial and Approbation—Division of Labour in the Examination—Traditional History Concluded—Attention directed to Implements and Emblems—Ornaments of a Lodge—The Three Grand Masters—Many Lodges omit the latter portion of the Traditional History—This should not be—A lame and impotent Conclusion, and an Injustice to the Candidate.

WHEN a Candidate for the Third Degree is conducted to the door of the Lodge, the K......s of the Second Degree are given, constituting an alarm. The reason for this is given on page 76. After the Prayer, he has to make three perambulations. During the first circuit, he has to prove to the brethren, through an examination conducted by the Junior Warden, that he has been regularly initiated into Freemasonry. During the second round he has to prove to the Senior Warden that he has been duly passed in the Second, or Fellow-Craft's Degree. He is then halted on the North side of the Senior Warden's pedestal, and the brethren are requested to observe that he 'is about to pass in view before them, to show that he is properly prepared.' During the third round the Candidate has to prove to the Senior Warden that he is in possession of the P.... G.... and the P.... W.... leading from the Second to the Third Degree.

Now, inasmuch as it is the invariable rule in each Degree that the Candidate shall undergo *one* examination, no more, and no less, during *each* of these preliminary perambulations, it is clear that the rule laid down on page 115 is the correct rule ; namely, that there shall be one perambulation for the First Degree, and no more ; two for the Second Degree, no more and no less ; and three for the Third Degree, no more and no less.

It is true the Candidate for Initiation is challenged twice in going once round the Lodge, but this is not really an exception to the rule ; he has only to undergo the *one examination* twice repeated, comprising the same questions and answers as were given at the door of the Lodge. This is inevitable and indispensable if the theory of the three doors (one real and two imaginary) be maintained. This is fully explained on page 121.

All sorts of devices are resorted to, to represent *that* over which the Candidate has to pass, in advancing from West to East. In one Lodge, well known to the writer, the Tyler was always brought in, and was made to take the necessary position, and was covered up. In a very great number of Lodges at the present time, a canvas painted to represent *a coffin* of the modern shape is used. This utterly fails to represent the thing signified, which is an O...n G...e ; besides being at variance with the custom of the East, as we have shown on page 53.

A Tracing Board for the Third Degree which the writer occasionally sees, and which was painted by a local artist, is a fair representation of an O...n G...e, with *something*, dim and indistinct, lying in it ; the very beau ideal of a Third Tracing Board ; an accurate presentment of the event commemorated, as distinguished from the picture of a modern coffin lid, which does duty for a Tracing Board in the vast majority of Lodges ; a travesty of the scene which is the central object of the Third Degree.

The Tracing Board mentioned in the preceding paragraph is framed and hung upon the wall of the Lodge room, and it cannot therefore be used, as it otherwise might be, in 'the proper method of advancing from West to East.' Inexpensive substitutes may easily be found ; the least costly, perhaps, is a piece of black cloth or linen (a parallelogram of course, as a G...e would be) about six feet by two ; a white, or light gray border round it, in order to define its limits, is desirable, considering the state of the Lodge at the time.

A juvenile brother, probably more witty than wise, once suggested that the Senior Deacon, when instructing the Candidate in 'the method of advancing,' etc., might, in addition to the customary instruction, add the words ' *as though you were skating on the outer edge.'* The idea was apt but irreverent, only excusable as coming from an Undergraduate.

The remarks made upon the Obligation in the First and in the Second Degrees apply equally to that of the Third Degree ; and even with greater force as to the words, ' Rise, duly obligated Master Mason ;' because immediately afterwards the Candidate is told that there awaits him ' that last and greatest trial, *by which alone* he can be admitted to a participation in the S.... of the Third Degree.'   It is clear, therefore, that until he has passed through this preliminary ordeal, and has been entrusted with the S..., and has been invested with the Apron, he has no right to be called a Master Mason.

We will repeat the hypothetical case, stated in the remarks upon this subject in the First Degree. Suppose that from sudden illness, or any other cause, the Candidate were to leave the Lodge immediately after the Obligation ; would he be received at any future time as a Master Mason ?   He could not prove himself in any way, he would not be admitted to any Lodge above the Fellow-Craft's Degree.   At the time when he is bidden to rise he is, and will be for a short time (until he is invested), in a state of probation ; therefore the better form of words would be, ' Rise, duly-obligated Probationer in the Third Degree.' The word Probationer is of ancient date.   Anyone wishing to devote himself to a Monastic life, was admitted at first as a Probationer, or a Novice, as the case might be ; and he so remained for a time, before he took the final vows of the Order.   (For some remarks upon the Obligation see Appendix I, page 257.)

It will be found to be convenient, immediately after the Candidate has been bidden to rise, for the Wardens to leave their places, bringing the L... and the P...R..., and silently to take the places of the Deacons. If the change be made at a later stage—as is often done—when the Worshipful Master breaks off in the narrative, and with almost startling abruptness says, ' Brother Wardens,' there ensues a certain degree of movement which the Candidate cannot understand, and which to a great extent distracts his attention from the Master's address, and the narrative of the Traditional History ; with the possibility of increasing the then very probable tension of his nerves. This is altogether undesirable, entirely purposeless, and consequently unnecessary.

It will be found far better to make the change when the position of the Candidate himself is changed, because at that moment he will be moved (stepping backwards) to the foot of the |⎯⎯⎯| ; leaving ample space in the front of the pedestal, where the Worshipful Master will stand when he comes to that portion of the narrative (involving action on his part) which will compel him to leave his place, and to stand upon the floor facing the Candidate.

The Wardens should be especially careful not to perform their respective functions too soon ; a good deal has to be said before the moment for action arrives. Each Warden should wait for the cue, or catch-word, namely ' Temple.' The instant the Worshipful Master utters that word, the Junior Warden performs his duty ; and, in accordance with the words which precede ' Temple,' namely, 'glanced... R...

T...e,' he lightly applies the Plumb-rule in the same (glancing) manner ; and in his turn, at the same word, the Senior Warden applies the Level lightly, in the same way.

Immediately before the final action, the Senior Warden may place his right foot behind the heels of the Candidate, and in a whisper caution him to be perfectly passive. If, as sometimes happens, the Candidate be allowed to step backward, he cannot be placed where preparation has been made for him. One Ritual, in a note, says, 'The S. W. stands on the left of the Can., the J. W. on his right, and direct him to c... his f....' It is better that the Candidate should not be asked to change his posture, and thus be caused to wonder what is coming next. The simple silent action of the right foot of the Senior Warden fully answers the purpose ; it renders a backward step impracticable.

If, as we have previously asserted, it be true etiquette to do the right thing in the right way, at the right time, and in the right place, then the details of position and of action which we have here given are not beyond the scope of a treatise upon the Etiquette of Freemasonry which is intended to be carried through upon the lines laid down in the opening Chapter. These details, perfectly intelligible, and easy of accomplishment as they are, still require considerable care; and it is not too much to expect of the three Principal Officers of a Lodge that they should exercise the care necessary to prevent a hitch or a fiasco in that which is really the central point of the whole Ceremony.

After the Candidate is R...d he should be placed well back on the North side of the Lodge, and facing South, having the Emblems of M. on his left hand and the representation of the G. on his right; so that in the address which follows, the Worshipful Master may direct his attention to the one and the other without a change of position.

When the Master communicates the S... of this Degree, the Candidate is instructed to advance first as an Entered Apprentice, next as a Fellow-Craft, and then to take another S... P.... The caution about the shortness of the P..., always given in each Degree, is too little insisted upon, and is too often entirely disregarded, an ordinary P... being usually taken by the Candidate unchecked by the Deacons. The result in this Degree of the P...s, given as ordinarily, is that, as the Candidate advances, the Master must step back in a somewhat undignified manner, until— as sometimes occurs—he is driven to the extreme South side of the Lodge.

The Candidate should, from the commencement, be instructed that in every case the P... intended is not a P... as usually understood, that little more than a mere movement of the f...t is required, three to six inches being ample in every Degree. We may imagine the result when the Brethren round the Lodge are commanded to stand to order, and each accompanies the S...n with the S...p (as he always should), if some took a s... of twelve inches, others of eighteen, and others of twenty-four; the line would be broken, and the effect would be absurd. In the case of standing to order, especially, the rule of a simple movement of the f... should be strictly observed.

After the Worshipful Master has communicated the s...s, the frequent—not the universal—custom is to give the Candidate permission 'to retire in order,' etc. This permission is not given in the two previous Degrees until the Novice or Probationer has been conducted to the Wardens for trial and approbation.* It would be more in accordance with the precedent established in those Degrees if a precisely similar course were followed in the Third Degree. Why should it not be so? It would be difficult to give a reason to the contrary. By sending the Candidate out of the Lodge thus prematurely there is a breach in the continuity of the ceremony, which is undesirable, to say the least of it, and apparently purposeless and inexplicable.

The ceremony is made to assimilate to the two preceding it, and is completed up to the same point if, immediately after the Candidate has been entrusted with the S..., the Master instructs the Deacons to 'conduct him to the Wardens for trial and approba-

---

* Many prefer here the word 'probation,' and with some good reasons for the preference. Probation is the act of proving, and when the Candidate is conducted to the Wardens they *try* him and *prove* him. When, in opening the Lodge in the Second and Third Degrees, the Junior Warden is asked, 'Are you a Fellow-Craft Freemason?'—or 'Are you a Master Mason?'—he answers, 'I am, Worshipful Master; *try me* and *prove me*. Here then also we have *trial* and *probation*. The word approbation certainly applies, because the Wardens imply *approbation* when they bid the Novice or Probationer to 'pass.' It needs no great amount of dialectic skill to be able—like Midshipman Easy—to argue on both sides of the question; an argument perhaps no more profitable than to discuss

'. . . . The difference there be
'Twixt tweedledum and tweedledee.'

tion.' In order to expedite the examination there may be a division of labour, the Junior taking the S...p and the three ordinary S...s, and the Senior (stepping on to the floor) omitting the S...s and taking the Five P...s of F...p and the W...d. The probationer is then in the proper place to be presented and invested; the Working Tools are presented, and the ceremony is so far complete. The *newly-made Master Mason* is instructed to salute the Worshipful Master, and he is then conducted out of the Lodge.

When the newly-raised Brother is brought back to the Lodge, the remaining portion of the Traditional History should always, if possible, be narrated, the implements with which H. A. B. was S. should be mentioned, and attention should be directed to the Emblems of M... After this, the remaining two of the S...s are communicated. Some of the Rituals include among the Emblems of M... the C.... This is a great mistake; they were unknown in the East before and after the date assumed in the Ceremony. The use of the winding-sheet was universal. No allusion ought to be made to 'the Ornaments of a Master Masons' Lodge;' there is no foundation in the Bible for the descriptions given of 'the Porch, the Dormer, and the Square Pavement;' they never had an existence except in the imagination of the old compilers of the Ritual. See Appendix J, page 260, wherein also the question of the 're-interment' is mentioned.

It is not an infrequent occurrence to hear H. A. B. alluded to as 'our Master.' If we are to be guided by the teaching of a higher Degree, the proper title would be our Grand Master, he having been one of the three *Grand* Masters (the others being Solomon, King of Israel, and Hiram, King of Tyre) who presided over the Craft during the building of the Temple.

In Lodges here and there scattered about the country the latter portion of the Traditional History is seldom or never narrated; in fact, in very many Lodges the Degree is too often given with maimed rites. This should not be. The Candidate is entitled to know all that we in the ceremonies have to teach, and if he be of an inquiring mind, and if the narrative, etc., be not completed, he will be led to consider that the ceremony, which began with great solemnity, and with a most interesting historical narrative, had come to an abrupt and a very lame and impotent conclusion. An imperfect or ill conducted performance of the ceremonies is an injustice to the Candidate and to Freemasonry itself.

CHAPTER XVIII.

MODE OF SALUTING, AND OTHER MATTERS.

Manner of Saluting differs greatly—The Correct Form on Entering—Perhaps too Elaborate on Leaving—But there is no Law on the Subject—A Model Master of a Lodge—W. M. Greeting a Visitor—W. M.'s Return Salute to Members—Reception of a Brother Visitor of High Rank—J. W. to announce First Report—But may be Authorised to take further Reports—But 'Alarms' not Delegated—Broad Distinction between 'Report' and 'Alarm'—Announcement of Brethren and Visitors—A superfluous Caution—Things to be Nipped in the Bud—The Use of the Gavel—Wardens should Always be Ready—Too great Energy often Displayed—A Useful Precaution to save the Pedestal from the Gavel—The W. M.'s Inquiry (thrice) as to whether any Brother has a Proposition—Questions should be Reserved until after the Ceremonial Business—Reasons given—The good of Free-masonry.

THE manner of saluting the Worshipful Master by Brethren who enter the Lodge when it is opened in the Second or the Third Degree differs greatly in various Lodges, and even among members of the same Lodge.

By far the greater number of Brethren give the S...n of the then Degree, with or without (too often without) the S...p. Others give the number of S...ps (unaccompanied by any S...n) according to the Degree in which the Lodge may be, finishing with the S...n of the then Degree. Others, again, beginning with both the S...p and the S...n of an

Entered Apprentice, will proceed to give the S...p and the S...n of a Fellow-Craft, and, if the Lodge be in the Third Degree, they will give the S...p and the P...l S...n of a Master Mason.

Probably the latter is technically the correct form; the objection to it is that it gives trouble and takes up time (very little of either). On the other hand, we have in support of the custom the fact that in communicating the S...s of the Second Degree the Worshipful Master always instructs the Candidate to advance first as an Entered Apprentice before the S...s of the Second Degree are communicated; and in the Third Degree the Candidate is instructed to advance first as an Entered Apprentice, then as a Fellow-Craft, previously to his being entrusted with the S...s of the Third Degree.

When the Candidate in the Second or the Third Degree is presented to the Wardens 'for trial and approbation,' a precisely similar course is followed; he is instructed to advance first as an Entered Apprentice and then to work upward to the S...s of the Second or the Third Degree as the case may be.

These precedents may be taken to show that in all cases the S...n of a Fellow-Craft should be led up to by the S...p and S...n of an Entered Apprentice, and that the S...n of a Master Mason should be preceded by the S...ps and the S...ns of the two previous Degrees. This may, by some Brethren, be considered somewhat too pedantic for general adoption upon entering the Lodge; it appears, nevertheless, to be the correct form. It may, however, well be thought to be too elaborate a performance to be gone through on leaving the Lodge. There is no law upon the subject, and the custom is not sufficiently established either way to enable one to dogmatise upon it.

A model Master of a Lodge, and one of the most thoroughly letter-perfect workers of the century, Brother Richard James Spiers,* some time Deputy Provincial Grand Master of Oxfordshire, whenever he occupied the chair of the Alfred Lodge (in which he was initiated, and of which he remained a Member to the last), always, upon the admission of a visitor from another Lodge, said: 'I greet you well, Brother A. B.' This form of greeting would appear to be of ancient date; it has a good old Masonic flavour about it; it is courteous to a visitor as distinguished from a Member of the Lodge. It is a form of welcome quite distinct from anything one hears in the outer world. This, or some other equally courteous greeting to visitors is worthy of observance in Lodges generally.

When a Member of the Lodge enters or leaves the Lodge, and salutes according to the then Degree, it is a simple act of courtesy for the Worshipful Master to salute him in return. It is unnecessary for the Master to utter any words of welcome to a Member of the Lodge, that form of greeting being reserved for visitors only.

* The author of this work was one of some half-dozen who occasionally—perhaps three or four times in a year—worked the seven sections of the First Lecture. Brother Spiers always occupied the Master's chair upon those occasions, and he gave the whole of the questions, from the beginning to the end, without any note or scrap of memorandum to assist him. He never hesitated, never made a mistake nor an omission. It was a marvellous effort of memory, probably very rarely equalled; it could not be surpassed in that way, because it was perfection itself.

It is, perhaps, unnecessary to mention that in the case of a Brother of high rank in Grand Lodge, or Provincial or District Grand Lodge, visiting a Lodge other than his own, the Brethren should all rise, and should answer his salutation by a corresponding S..., remaining standing until their visitor has taken his seat.

At the first report after the Lodge is opened, the Junior Warden should always announce that report to the Worshipful Master as he has received it from the Inner Guard; the Master would then say, ' You will inquire who seeks admission,' and he may add, ' You will take the reports for the remainder of the evening.' Thenceforward the Junior Warden ceases to forward the reports to the Worshipful Master ; having been duly authorized, he at once, in every case, directs the Inner Guard to ' see who seeks admission.'

This delegated authority relates to *reports* only ; it does not include an *alarm*. When an alarm is sounded in either Degree, the Junior Warden, after receiving notice thereof from the Inner Guard, conveys the announcement to the Worshipful Master in the proper form.

The difference of procedure pointed out in the two preceding paragraphs will show the indispensable necessity of the Tyler and of the Inner Guard being thoroughly conversant with the broad distinction between the ' report ' and the ' alarm ' in each Degree, because any mistake or confusion between the two must inevitably lead to confusion in the Lodge.

When two or more Brethren are announced it is

not necessary to give the names of all; on the other hand, it is not right to omit the mention of any name, as one too often hears, in this way: ' Several Brethren seek admission.' A more correct form is for the Tyler to say: ' Brother A. B. and other Brethren seek admission,' and the Inner Guard will use the same form of words. If a visitor happen to be one of the group, he should be allowed to go first, and, as a matter of course, his name would be announced.

The Junior Warden's reply to the announcement is: ' Admit him,' or 'them,' or 'You will admit him,' or them,' as the case may be. This is the rule. In some Lodges, however (presumably, very few), the Junior Warden uses this formula: ' Admit him, *if properly clothed.*' The last three words are clearly superfluous, and worse, they imply a doubt of the efficiency of the Tyler and of the Inner Guard. It is extremely improbable that, if the Brother seeking admission were not ' properly clothed,' the fact would escape the vigilance of both those Officers.

The use of these additional words subserves no useful end or purpose ; it is one of those redundant forms of expression which have crept into the working of the Lodges in which they are used, no one knows whence, or how, or why. Masters of Lodges and Directors of Ceremonies should always be especially careful to nip in the bud the first introduction of all superfluous and meaningless phrases and forms of expression, even as, with the Gavel, the Entered Apprentice is taught ' to knock off all superfluous knobs and excrescences.'

In connection with the Gavel we may mention that it is desirable that the Wardens should be always ready to answer the K....k of the Worshipful Master. For this purpose, they should always have the Gavel in their hand. If it be laid upon the pedestal an appreciable space of time is occupied in taking it up, and the three knocks do not follow in the moderately quick order that is desirable.

Much unnecessary energy is too often displayed in the use of the Gavel. One sometimes hears a succession of sounding blows that would not discredit Thor himself, emitting sounds that may be heard far beyond the Lodge room.* This is objectionable, for more than one obvious reason. A moderately-sharp *tap*, and not a heavy blow, is all that is required upon any occasion.†

While the Lodge is open in the First Degree, at certain convenient times, the Worshipful Master gives one K....k, which is followed by the Wardens; he then rises and says : ' I rise to inquire if any Brother has a proposition to make for the good of Freemasonry in general, or of this Lodge in particular, for the first time ?' Or he may use the shorter form of words: ' Has any Brother a proposition to make for the good of Freemasonry in general, or of this Lodge in

---

* This forcible use of the Gavel may be an instance of heredity, showing a descent from a Scandinavian ancestry ; presumably worshippers of Thor, the wielder of the wonderful hammer !

† A very useful precaution for securing the top of the pedestal from injury is to provide (for each pedestal) a flat piece of wood —presumably oak like the pedestal—say five or six inches square and three-fourths of an inch thick, the under-side covered with cloth. This will receive the indentations inevitably consequent upon the repeated taps, or (worse) the blows of the Gavel.

particular?' After an interval of time the K......s are given as before, and the question is repeated, ending with the words, 'for the second time.' Again, after an interval, the K......s and the question are repeated 'for the third time.'

It is specially to be noted that the Master asks these questions only when the Lodge is opened in the First Degree, and for a very sufficient reason. In the discussion of any motion, or of any subject that may come up during the meeting of the Lodge, an Entered Apprentice, who is a subscribing member, has as clear a right to vote upon the matter under discussion as any other member of the Lodge. For this reason the questions mentioned in the preceding paragraph are generally reserved until after the ceremonial business of the Lodge has been disposed of.

Another advantage is gained by delaying discussions, and the proposition of Candidates, or of joining members, until the later portion of the sitting, namely, that Brethren whose 'public or private avocations' have precluded the possibility of an early attendance at the Lodge, will probably have arrived, and they may then be enabled to make any proposition, or to take a part in any deliberation, or discussion, having for its object 'the good of Freemasonry in general, or of their own Lodge in particular.'

CHAPTER XIX.

'HEARTY GOOD WISHES.'

Some correspondence has recently (1890) appeared in *The Freemason* upon the question of the right of visitors to tender to the Lodge in which they are guests 'Hearty good wishes' from the Lodges of which they are severally members. Most of the letters are of an inquiring character; the respective writers want to know if they have, or have not, been rightly informed as to Grand Lodge having expressed an opinion 'unfavourable to the continuance of the custom.' Grand Lodge has expressed no opinion favourable, or otherwise, upon the subject.

The actual facts are as follows: The opinion of the late Grand Registrar of the Order was taken upon the question, and he gave it to this effect: 'that no

Brother has the right to convey the good wishes, hearty or otherwise, of his own Lodge to any other Lodge without the permission of his own Worshipful Master.' This is authentic ; the source from which the information has been derived is unimpeachable, the words between the commas are the very words of the late lamented Brother McIntyre, but whether he qualified his opinion in any way we have no know-ledge.

The foregoing inquiry, and the opinion given in reply, constitute the whole that has occurred in con-nection with this question ; it is therefore a great mistake to suppose that Grand Lodge disapproves of the practice of ' Hearty good wishes,' as evidently is the impression of several of the writers of the letters which have appeared in *The Freemason.* Grand Lodge has never discussed the subject.

We should not lose sight of the fact that our late Grand Registrar was a lawyer, a Q.C., and if the question were put to him as a point of law, and of abstract right, he would give an opinion in accordance with the *strict letter of the law,* as the form of his answer (if it were really as laconic as it is made to appear) would seem to show.

The fact of Brother McIntyre's opinion having been asked upon this subject almost forces us to the con-clusion that this is a fad, or a crotchet, of the inquirer ; and the opinion given in reply is after all only the judgment of one man, learned in the law, who having been asked a question of law, answered according to law, strictly and literally.

An old Latin proverb runs thus: ' Summum jus est

summa injuria ' (' Extreme law is extreme injustice '),
which means that certain acts which may be right
according to law may become a grievous wrong in
practice, as in the case of a man who bequeaths his
property to charities, or otherwise, leaving his family
destitute.   In such cases the Courts intervene, and
pronounce against the will, although the law holds
that a man may do as he will with his own.

We may take the case of the owner of an estate ;
it is undoubtedly his by law, but by prescription and
immemorial usage the public have a right of way
across a portion of the property.   The owner cannot
stop the road or footpath, although his lawful owner-
ship of every yard of the road or path is indisputable.
Cases have often occurred of the owners of estates
endeavouring to exclude the public from the ancient
ways across their properties, as in the Highlands of
Scotland, and quite recently in the Lake district ;
but as a rule the rights of the public have been
successfully maintained.

As in the case of the right of way here cited, we
have in favour of our ancient custom the ' Lex non
scripta,' the unwritten law, sanctioned by precedent
and by immemorial usage.   Speaking from an experience of close upon half a century in Freemasonry,
during which time many Lodges have been visited
in various provinces, the writer can bear witness that
the custom during that period, at least, has been
universal ; there has been no difference in the practice,
no break in its continuity, no exception to its univer-
sality ; it has, like a vigorous forest tree, struck its
roots deep, and spread its branches wide ; it should

not, and will not, be uprooted upon no stronger grounds than the opinion of one man, however eminent, and however worthy of respect and reverence he may have been.

That the late Grand Registrar used the words imputed to him there can be no shadow of doubt whatever; but we may well doubt that he uttered those words without any modification or qualification of any kind. He was a practical man, and a good Freemason; and it is not only possible, but quite probable, that he might have taken a practical common-sense view of the question. In that case his answer to his interviewers would be something of this kind: 'Well, if you ask me if a brother has *the right* to speak on behalf of his Lodge, I reply that *by law* he has not the right, except with the permission of the Master; nevertheless, it is an ancient custom, kindly, genial, fraternal, harmless in itself, and genuinely Masonic; it existed before we were born, it will endure long after we are buried; *you had better leave it alone.*'

'De minimis non curat lex' ('The law does not concern itself with trifling things'), and we may rest assured that Grand Lodge will never take this *small* matter into serious consideration. We heard of late —in some debates in the House of Commons—of 'Grandmotherly legislation'; of this character would be any attempt to carry in Grand Lodge any motion having for its object the abolition of our time-honoured custom of each visiting brother tendering, on behalf of his Lodge, and for himself, 'Hearty good wishes' to the Lodge in which he is a guest at the time.

We may consider what would be the effect of such

a motion if it were carried ; we should see repeatedly the anomaly of some visitors who had obtained permission from the Masters of their respective Lodges rising in their places, and offering 'hearty good wishes' as of old, while others, who had neglected to ask the (then) necessary permission, would be condemned to a silence painful to themselves and discourteous to the visited Lodge.

Permissive legislation is always objectionable, because it always involves anomalies ; witness the operation of the Maine liquor law in America, where the inhabitants of a State in which the law is in force have only to go into a neighbouring State which has not adopted the law and they may drink their fill. Similarly in Wales, the inhabitants of the border in Flintshire have (or had) only to go into Cheshire, posing as *bonâ fide* travellers, and, like Ben Backstay in the old sea song, they could 'get tipsy unto their hearts' content.'

We may also quote the result of Sir William Charley's Act, which places in the hands of the governing bodies in towns the power either to allow or forbid the use of steam-whistles, and 'buzzards,' and other such implements of torture. In one manufacturing town in the north—well-known to the writer —in which the majority of those in authority are connected with the mills, steam-whistles, etc., are allowed to be used. The result is that the night (or, rather, the early morning from *five to six*) is made hideous with the ceaseless din of whistles shrieking in every direction, and every conceivable key, to the discomfort of light sleepers and to the injury of invalids.

In the neighbouring (almost adjoining) town steam-whistles and all such abominations *are not* permitted to be used at any time, and the inhabitants can sleep in peace. This is the result of permissive legislation. The result of such legislation with regard to ' hearty good wishes' would be equally anomalous and absurd. If a thing be right in itself it should be done without restriction ; if it be wrong, it should be forbidden without exception.

Since the foregoing paragraphs were written a letter has appeared in *The Freemason* singularly confirming the opinion that anomalies would be observed with regard to this subject. The letter runs thus :

' I agree with your correspondent (P. M.) that it would be convenient to know if Grand Lodge objects to the familiar "hearty good wishes" so often heard from the visitor. I hear that at a recent Installation meeting, and in presence of a distinguished Officer of Grand Lodge, the newly-installed Worshipful Master told the visitors, in reply to their "hearty good wishes," that they were "out of order." In contradistinction from this, I was present at an Installation meeting a few days ago, when a distinguished Past Grand Treasurer was *one of the first* to offer to the Worshipful Master "hearty good wishes." "Who shall decide when doctors disagree ?"

' (Signed)

' PUZZLED P. M.'

We have discussed this subject at considerable length, because this is not the first time (it will probably not be the last) when an expression of individual opinion on the part of some Officer of rank in Grand Lodge has been repeated, or perhaps we may venture to say has been carefully disseminated, and as it has been passed from one to another, gathering strength as it went on, it has at last been believed to be the opinion of Grand Lodge. This accurately describes the course of the present scare (it is certainly a false alarm) about 'hearty good wishes'; the opinion of one or two Members of Grand Lodge has been promulgated, and believed in, as an edict of Grand Lodge, while Grand Lodge as a body has never discussed the question, and knows nothing about it.

Brethren should not be too ready to believe the assertion that Grand Lodge wills this, or disapproves of that; the truth or otherwise of such statements is to be discovered without much difficulty through the proper official channels, and in cases of grave doubt or difficulty no Brother need hesitate to make inquiry; he may be sure of a courteous reply, always presuming that the case is of importance. Perhaps we may say generally that the Secretary of a Lodge would in most cases be the best channel of communication for obtaining information as to all matters affecting the interests of the Craft.

In the extremely improbable event of Grand Lodge legislating in a way adverse to the good old custom, it would not be too much to expect that every Lodge should be notified of the change; until that time shall have arrived we may safely go on in the old way, giving and receiving 'hearty good wishes,' as the custom has been ' from a time of which the memory of man runneth not to the contrary.'*

* The author wrote a letter upon this subject ; it was inserted in *The Freemason* of April 12th, 1890.

The following paragraph appeared in *The Freemason* of June 14th, 1890—if the old custom is doomed (which we doubt) it will ' die hard ': ' It may interest those Brethren who took part in the recent discussion in our columns on " Hearty Good Wishes " to know that we have it on the authority of Bro. Dr. Hill Drury, Secretary of the Universities' Lodge, that at the consecration of that Lodge in February last the representatives of no less than forty-four Lodges tendered their " Hearty Good Wishes." '

CHAPTER XX.

SOME MATTERS OF GENERAL DETAIL.

Time of Offering ' Hearty Good Wishes'—Order of Precedence according to Masonic Rank—When Propositions should be made—Notices of Motion should be set forth in the Summons—Order in which the Ceremonies should be Performed—Good Reasons for the Rule—Greater Interest in the Ceremony of Initiation—Impression upon the Candidate—First Ceremony better Understood and Appreciated after a Second Performance—A curious Psychological Study—Ceremony should be Well Conducted—A Complaint—Abbreviations—Proper Form of Addressing the W. M.—A Case of Initials that might be Misinterpreted.

ASSUMING—as we reasonably may—that the custom discussed in the previous chapter has not been, and will not be, discontinued to any appreciable extent in Lodges generally, we may consider the proper time, or times, at which that custom may be conveniently practised. There is no positive, no general, still less universal, rule upon the subject. In certain Lodges the rule observed is as follows. After the Worshipful Master has asked if '... any brother has a proposition to make . . . for the first time,' Grand Lodge Officers (if any be present) offer ' hearty good wishes from the Grand Lodge of England'; at the second time of asking, Provincial or District Grand Officers present 'hearty good wishes' from their respective Provinces or Districts ; at the third time of asking, Members of

Private or Military Lodges tender 'hearty good wishes' from their several Lodges.

The rule set forth in the previous paragraph is a reasonable one; it is in accordance with the fitness of things that gradations of rank should be assigned their several periods, in which Brethren holding the highest positions should be first heard; next those in the second grade, and last those visitors who have no Grand or Provincial or District rank. This rule promotes order and regularity in this portion of the proceedings in the Lodge, and 'the Etiquette of Freemasonry' demands that the order of precedence, according to Masonic Rank, should be strictly observed in this respect as in all others.

As a general rule the question—thrice repeated— 'Has any brother a proposition to make?' etc., is deferred until after the conclusion of the Ceremonies, in order that Brethren arriving late may be present to take a part—if they wish to do so—in any discussion that may arise; and as the Lodge will have been closed down to the First Degree, 'Brethren in the inferior Degrees' may vote in any division which may take place.

After the question has been asked for the third time, propositions of Candidates for Initiation or as joining Members are usually made; notices of motions to be made at a future meeting are given, and motions of which notice had been given at a previous meeting are brought forward and discussed. It is generally understood that notice of any motion of *more than minor importance* should be given at a regular meeting of the Lodge, and that the motion itself should be set forth in the circular convoking the meeting at which it is to be brought forward. It is obvious that Brethren who were not present when the notice was given, have a clear right to be duly notified by circular of the terms and scope of the motion, and of the meeting at which it is to be discussed.

A good rule is observed in many—perhaps the majority — of Lodges, in the order in which the ceremonies are performed. If Initiations, Passings, and Raisings have to be performed at any one meeting, the Raisings are taken first, the Passings next, and the Initiations last. Good reasons can be assigned for this regulation; *inter alia*, the number of Brethren present is, as a rule, greater towards the end of the meeting than at the beginning, and consequently the Lodge is at its best in point of appearance; therefore it is calculated to make a better impression upon the mind of the Candidates than would a possibly ' beggarly array ' of empty chairs.

Brethren generally evince a warmer interest in, and will make more strenuous efforts to be present at, the ceremony of Initiation than at either of the other two. It is naturally to be expected that this would be the case, because it is the formal reception of a new member into our Order, and most of us feel an excusable curiosity to see what manner of man the Candidate is, and how he will conduct himself under the entirely new circumstances in which he will find himself placed.

Moore, in ' The Fire-Worshippers ' in Lalla Rookh, thus sings of Hinda :

'Strange and new
Is all that meets her wandering view;
Upon a galliot's deck she lies.'

This aptly describes the condition of the Candidate during the Ceremony of Initiation; all that he hears and sees is 'strange and new,' and may we be pardoned for completing the simile by saying that, as far as a clear comprehension of the Ceremony is concerned, he is 'very much at sea' generally.

We have most of us heard newly-initiated Brethren express themselves to the effect that they understood and appreciated the Ceremony of Initiation in far greater measure after having witnessed and heard it performed a second time than they did at their own Initiation. Naturally this would be the case; the whole surrounding circumstances, the action, the moral teaching, even the phraseology of the Ceremony, being so far removed from anything within the range of their experience in the outer world, so different from any ' opinion preconceived' of that which actually takes place in the Lodge.

A very curious psychological study would be produced by a transcript of the various impressions made upon the minds of the majority of the newly-initiated Members of our Order by the First Ceremony. It may be assumed generally that those impressions —favourable or the reverse—would be just in accordance with the degree of carefulness, accuracy, and impressiveness (or with the absence of those qualities) with which the Ceremony had in each case been performed. Instances of very varied results, consequent upon the Ceremony having been well or ill conducted, are within the experience of perhaps every member of mature years among us.

' A tree is known by its fruits,' and increasingly numerous as our Fraternity is, we may conclude that, as a general rule, the seed sown in our Lodges is good seed, well planted, well nourished, or it would not—as it has done, and is doing—' take root downward, and bear fruit upward, a hundredfold,' as the number of new Lodges year by year added to the registry of the Grand Lodge abundantly testifies. Nevertheless in very many Lodges complaint is made of the falling away of good men and Brethren from our midst, and of the coldness and apathy of many who retain their membership, but whose visits to the Lodge are few and far between. This is perhaps inevitable. It is not given to everyone to appreciate at its proper value our excellent Institution, or to derive ' profit and pleasure ' from its moral teaching.

Everyone who studies any Ritual of the Craft will have noticed that initial letters, representing the names of the Officers, are generally used, as, for example, W. M., S. W., J. W., and so on to I. G. These, however, are only used for the sake of brevity, in order to save space. No abbreviations of any kind should be used in the Lodge at any time, upon any occasion. We hear occasionally the Worshipful Master addressed as W. M., not in the opening and closing of the Lodge, or during the Ceremonies, but in addressing the Master at any other period during the meeting. One sometimes hears the Master addressed as ' Worshipful.' This is altogether inexcusable, being totally devoid of the respect due to the high position which the Master holds.

Frequently Past Masters may be heard to address the Worshipful Master as 'Worshipful Sir,' thus implying (we presume) the perfect equality of themselves with the Master. This is a mistaken idea altogether. The Worshipful Master, during the period of his tenure of that Office, is paramount over all, over every member of the Lodge, be he Past Master or Entered Apprentice; there is no exception to this rule.

Unfortunately habits of this kind are contagious, and we hear occasionally a Junior Warden (not being a Past Master) reply, 'I am, Worshipful Sir;' and others below the rank even of Junior Warden are apt to follow the bad example. All such deviations from established rule and order, and from the etiquette of the Lodge, should be strictly guarded against and repressed, whoever may be the offender in this respect, and whatever may be his status in the Lodge.

As a title implying equality of rank, the term may be admissible in the case of one Past Master addressing another, but even then 'Worshipful Brother' would be a better term. 'Sir' belongs to the outer world, it has no flavour of Freemasonry about it; it is better to leave it behind when we enter the Lodge. In the not improbable case of a Past Master acting as Master, and, *pro tempore*, another Past Master acting as Warden, or from any cause having to address the Acting Master, he should address him as 'Worshipful Master.' He is, for the time being, the representative of the Master of the Lodge, and thereby invested with

plenary powers, and fully entitled to the honours due
to the actual Worshipful Master.*

* The mention of initial letters signifying various Officers,
recalls to memory a circumstance not worthy of a place in the
body of this work, but the narration of which will perhaps be
excusable in a foot-note. During the first year of the writer's
bearing office in Oxford, the officers of the Lodge decided that
each should present to the Lodge some article in silver for the
table, a fork, a spoon, salts, and so on ; and each article had
engraved upon it the name of the donor and the initials of his
office. One brother, who had been in office as Inner Guard, but
in consequence of having to go abroad could not again take office,
said he would like to give something, and he would have his
name engraved upon it ; but as he could claim no rank but that
of Past Inner Guard, he preferred not to have the initials P. I. G.
to follow his name—it might be misinterpreted.

CHAPTER XXI.

'THE FESTIVE BOARD.'

The Duty of the Director of Ceremonies—Arrangement of Visitors and Members according to Rank—Certain Freedom of Choice generally Permissible—Still, Order and Regularity must not be Neglected—At Festivals a certain Degree of State and Ceremony should be Observed—Grace before and after Meat—Good old Masonic Forms of ' Asking a Blessing ' and ' Giving of Thanks '—Proposing Toasts—Forms will vary—Difference between Ordinary Meetings and Special Occasions —A good, useful, practical Programme for an Installation and Anniversary Banquet—' The Queen and the Craft '—The Old Form should be Retained—Visitors may require Special Mention—' The Honours '—Musical Performance—Division of Labour in the Matter of Toasts—When Smoking may be Enjoyed—A good old Custom—The E. A. Song.

THE etiquette of the table—or in old Masonic parlance 'the festive board'—differs in no material degree from the order and rules observed when a number of men meet and dine or sup together upon any occasion. The duty rests upon the Director of Ceremonies to see that the places at the table for visitors and for members are assigned in accordance with their rank in the Craft, allowing, of course, a certain degree of freedom of choice; that is to say, if a visitor be assigned a place at, or near the top of the table, and he prefers a seat beside the Brother who introduces him, or with whom he may be more or less intimate, his wish would, of course, be complied with. On the other hand, it would be bad taste for a Brother who bears no rank of any importance to aspire to occupy one of 'the uppermost rooms at feasts, lest a more honourable man than he come in,' etc.

There is, as a rule, more freedom from form and ceremony at the table after the ordinary meetings of the Lodge; still, order and regularity should not be neglected; rules should be observed as far as is compatible with freedom from unnecessary restraint, but they should not by any means be ignored. At Festivals (annual or other) a certain degree of state and ceremony should be observed, and the ordinary rules regulating the proceedings on such occasions should be more strictly enforced, and precedence should be given to rank and station in the Craft.

When Grace is said (that is, when it is not sung), if the Chaplain be present he should say it. One too often hears the hackneyed form, 'For what we are about to receive, the Lord make us truly thankful.' This does not embody the idea of 'Grace *before meat*,' expressed in the venerable formula of 'Asking a blessing;' it more nearly approaches the meaning of 'Grace after meat,' called of old, 'Giving of thanks.'

We have a good old Masonic form of 'Grace before meat,' and of 'Grace after meat,' which should not be allowed to fall into disuse. They run thus: 'May T. G. A. O. T. U. bless that which His bounty has provided for us. So mote it be,' and 'May T. G. A. O. T. U. give us grateful hearts, and supply the needs of others. So mote it be.' These are sufficiently brief, but at the same time they are very comprehensive; the first is in strict accordance with the old idea of 'asking a blessing,' and it at the same time acknowledges Him 'from Whom all blessings flow.' The 'Grace after meat' is not faultless in diction, but it is truly a 'giving of thanks,' and at the same time an aspiration (perhaps not very happily expressed) that those of our Brethren who are in need may have their wants supplied as amply as ours have been.

The custom of proposing certain regular toasts, and occasionally of drinking to the health of any particular Brother or Brethren who may be present, if not universal, is still general as of old; we have not heard of any exceptions ; *nor of any rumour, at present, that Grand Lodge disapproves of the practice.* The forms will necessarily vary to some extent in different Provinces or Districts, or even in neighbouring Lodges, but in their main features and in their order of sequence there is no great variation.

Even in the same Lodge some difference is generally made between the number of toasts given at an ordinary meeting and those included in the list intended for an Installation dinner, or an Anniversary, or any other special occasion. There is also not infrequently a difference observed in 'the honours' assigned to the toasts at a regular meeting and those in use on a special occasion ; that is to say, in the latter case the full honours should be given, while at a regular meeting simpler forms may be observed.

Where so great a variation of practice is certain to exist in different Lodges and different Provinces, one feels some degree of hesitation in even suggesting, and much more in dictating for general adoption, any programme of toasts. The utmost that can or ought to be done is to give a copy of a programme recently used at an Installation (and Anniversary banquet), with the honours assigned to each toast.

1. The King, Protector of the Craft. (Honours twenty and one, a pause between the twenty and the one; begin slowly, quicken as the honours proceed.)

One verse of 'God Save the King' (all standing).

2. Her Most Gracious Majesty the Queen, their Royal Highnesses the Prince and Princess of Wales, and the rest of the Royal Family. (Honours twenty and one. One verse or the whole of 'God Bless the Prince of Wales.')

3. His Royal Highness the Duke of Connaught and Strathearn, K.G., Most Worshipful Grand Master. (Honours twenty and one.)

4. The Lord Ampthill, G.C.S.I., G.C.I.E., Most Worshipful Pro-Grand Master. (Honours as for G.M.)

5. The Right Honourable Thomas Frederick Halsey, Right Worshipful Deputy Grand Master. (Honours three times seven.)

6. The Grand Masters of Scotland and Ireland. (Honours three times seven.)

7. Brother (name, and titles if any), Right Worshipful Provincial (or District) Grand Master of (insert the Province or District). (Honours seven times.)

8. Brother (name and rank), Very Worshipful Deputy Provincial (or District) Grand Master, and the Provincial (or District) Grand Officers present and past. (Honours three times three.)

9. The newly Installed Worshipful Master, Brother A. B. (Honours three times three.)

10. The Installing Master, Brother A. B. (and the

full titles of his rank in the Craft). The honours for this toast may be just the ordinary 'point-left-right,' etc., in the ordinary way, unless the Brother's rank entitles him to more.

11. The Visiting Brethren. (Honours as for 10.)

12. The Immediate Past Master and the other Past Masters of the Lodge. (Honours as for 10 and 11.)

13. The Masonic Charities. (Honours as last.)

14. The Senior and the Junior Warden, and the other Officers of the Lodge. (Honours as before.)

15. Prosperity to the Lodge (name), Number .... (Honours three times three.)

16. To all Poor and Distressed Freemasons (wherever dispersed over the face of Earth and Water). (Ordinary honours.)

It is no uncommon thing to find on programmes of Festivals and other occasions 'The King' as the first toast, without any reference to 'The Craft'; this is wrong. His Majesty is now 'Grand Protector of Freemasons'; it is, therefore, not 'derogatory to his dignity' to associate his name with that of the Craft, which he honours with his special protection.

In the united toast, we express at once our loyalty to the Throne, and our reverence for 'our ancient and honourable Fraternity.' 'The King and the Craft' is the original and very ancient form among Freemasons; whereas 'The King' alone is the form used at ordinary meetings in the outer world. We should retain the combined form by all means.

The toast No. 5 is not universally in use; with that exception there seems to be no toast in the list which could well be omitted upon state occasions. On the other hand, visitors may be present whose rank socially or Masonically may entitle them to special mention and a separate toast ; no hard and fast line can be or should be attempted to be drawn upon the subject. All that has been here aimed at is to give a good, useful, practical programme, fairly comprehensive and not wearisome.

With regard to 'the honours,' those herein specified have been obtained from a very efficient Provincial Grand Director of Ceremonies. They appear to have been well arranged, and are fairly proportioned to the individual rank of the several subjects of the various toasts. There is no authoritative rule and no universal custom ; the Worshipful Master and the Director of Ceremonies must always arrange the programme either in accordance with precedent in their Lodge or at their own discretion.

On Anniversaries or Installation banquets as a rule each toast is followed by a song or glee, or some musical performance. These are within the province of the Organist, and whatever may be arranged is set forth—each piece in it proper place—in the Programme. If the songs, glees, etc., be well selected, with some care as to their appropriateness to the toasts which they respectively follow, and if they be fairly well rendered, the entertainment as a whole will be successful and enjoyable, at least, let us hope, to the majority—to those who desire to be happy themselves, and, if it be in their power, to contribute to the happiness of their Brethren.

In some Lodges a custom exists for the Worshipful Master to propose —let us say—the first five toasts.

He then calls upon the Senior Warden to propose No. 6 (The Provincial or District Grand Master), and the Junior Warden to propose No. 7 (The Deputy Provincial or District Grand Master). After these two have been duly honoured, various Brethren selected by the Worshipful Master (assisted perhaps by the Director of Ceremonies) are requested to propose certain of the remaining toasts ; these being allotted to the several speakers according to their special fitness for the duty, derived, it may be, from an intimate knowledge of the subject of the toast with which each speaker is entrusted, or for other good and sufficient reasons.

In the Lodges mentioned in the last paragraph immediately after the toast of the Provincial or District Grand Master permission is given to the Brethren to smoke ; then, and not till then, cigars and other means and appliances for the enjoyment of the nicotian weed are brought into requisition.

No apology can be needed for the mention of tobacco in connection with the symposia of our Order, the habit is so generally, indeed universally, practised at our meetings. Still less need we hesitate to allude to the subject in these days, when, from the lordly club or social gathering in which princes occasionally disport themselves, down through all grades —to the working men's political or social club— ' smoking concerts ' are, as our American cousins would aptly say, in ' *full blast.*'

It is to be regretted that a good old custom, in general use some years ago, is now less observed than it formerly was. In the writer's earlier years in

Freemasonry, on every occasion when there had been an Initiation, immediately after the newly initiated Brother's health had been duly toasted, the Entered Apprentice's song was sung as a matter of course; indeed, the Brethren would as soon have thought of omitting the Charge as to forego the E. A. Song, with its chorus and the cordial hand-grasp all round during the singing of the last verse. Many of the older Brethren, and certainly the majority of the younger generation, would have considered the ceremony incomplete without the good old song.

(A copy of the E. A. Song, with a very few verbal corrections, will be found in the Appendix K, page 263.)

CHAPTER XXII.

SPEECHES AND THE CHARITIES.

In treating of the Etiquette of the table, it may be considered necessary that some mention should be made of the addresses of the Brethren in proposing the various toasts, and of the replies (returning thanks) of those whose healths—either singly or in connection with others—have formed the subjects of the personal toasts. A considerable amount of ridicule is cast upon the quality of post-prandial oratory, in fact, numbers of men advocate the entire abandonment of the practice, and that, as at military mess dinners, one toast only—'The King '—should be given.

It may well be doubted if the abolition, or even

the partial abandonment of the custom, or the serious curtailment of the lists of toasts which we have been accustomed to find upon the programmes of our Festivals, would be acceptable to any but a very small minority of the Members of the Craft.   The custom of giving toasts and of drinking healths at social gatherings, dinners, etc., in our own houses, is voted to be 'more honoured in the breach than the observance,' and is happily a thing of the past; but with us the case is different.   We profess to be, and we are, very properly tenacious of 'The ancient Landmarks of the Order.'   The custom of toasts at our so-called festive meetings is so old as to have become a social landmark—it should not be lightly abandoned, or tampered with to any serious extent.

At the ordinary meetings of the Lodge, it is not expected that the full complement of toasts shall be given, although, even then, a certain routine should be observed, such as : 'The King and the Craft'; 'The high dignitaries and the Rulers of the Order, supreme and subordinate'; 'The Worshipful Master,' and some others at discretion and in accordance with the probable duration of the sitting.   The list of toasts, however, should not be cut down to poor dimensions upon extraordinary occasions, such as Festivals, Installations, and so on, when large numbers—members and visitors—are expected to be present.

The kind, the manner, and the quality of the speeches one hears at the table at Masonic meetings differ, perhaps, quite as much as the speakers themselves differ the one from the other, and as the toasts vary in importance, and in general or individual interest. It is, therefore, clearly impossible to lay down rules for general adoption; to say, 'in proposing such a toast, your line of argument should be so, or so; and in replying to such a toast, your remarks should be couched in some such terms as these.' The attempt at dictation in these directions would be an impertinence, and would be as useless for general purposes as the examples of letters upon various subjects given in an old publication called 'The Polite Letter Writer.'

One hesitates to go so far even as to hint at, or to make the slightest suggestion upon, a subject so varying in all its surrounding circumstances as a list of toasts must necessarily be, comprising, as it does, subjects of the highest dignity and of world-wide interest, *e.g.*, 'The King and the Craft,' 'The Grand Master,' 'The Masonic Charities,' down to subjects of local interest, 'The Worshipful Master,' 'Success to Lodge Number ...,' and so on. Who shall prescribe—with any hope of even partial success—rules, or suggestions for their several introduction in speech? The author of this work will not make an attempt, so certain to result in a ridiculous failure.

A Demosthenes is not born every day. Nevertheless, in this and in the preceding century, the Law Courts and the political arena have produced their prodigies of eloquence; and among the members of our Order we may occasionally meet men capable of investing common subjects with the charm of their own fancy, affording an intellectual feast to their hearers. From such men we do not expect brief utterances—we should be disappointed with a short address—we expect something above the average in quantity as well as in quality, and generally we are not disappointed.

Except from men of superior attainments, and of unusual facility and happiness of expression, long speeches upon well-worn topics, such as the routine toasts given at our meetings, are a weariness of the flesh ; they should be studiously avoided. There are, however, certain toasts, such as the health of the Worshipful Master, particularly if by the performance of the duties of the lower Offices, and during his Mastership, he have shown exceptional zeal and ability ; in such a case a moderately lengthy address is not only permissible, but is eminently desirable.

Again, the toast wishing ' Success to the Masonic Charities ' is one that demands much more than a brief introduction. It is very desirable that at least ' once in every year ' the members of the Lodge should learn, from some well-informed brother, the excellent, the beneficent work, which year after year our various Charities are engaged in performing. Some well-selected, and not too minutely-detailed statistics, may well be given upon such occasions. The facts and figures thus produced tend to foster the virtue of Charity in the best possible way, namely, by convincing the brethren that the various Institutions are conducted with care and efficiency, that the large revenues are carefully administered, and that the results bear in all cases a full proportion to the means employed.

In many Provinces, every Lodge elects yearly a member, whose duty it is to attend to all matters connected with the Charities, both Metropolitan and Provincial, so far as the interests of their own Lodges are concerned. In the Provinces alluded to, there are Charities educational and otherwise, the benefits of which are restricted to the Provinces in which they exist; and the brother mentioned is the representative of his Lodge upon the Central Committee of the Province, which conducts the affairs of the Institution. In the case also of an application to the Board of Benevolence in London, the same brother goes to the meeting of the Board, to support the application, and to answer the searching questions which are always, and very properly, asked before the application is decided upon.

In many Lodges the same brother is re-elected year after year, with the good result that he becomes, as a rule, thoroughly well versed in the working of the Charities, and so is able to render eminent service to the Lodge. Who then can be a more 'fit and proper person' to propose the toast of 'The Masonic Charities' or perhaps, better still, to respond to the Toast? In the latter case some brother, selected for his fitness for the duty, might dilate at reasonable length upon 'the distinguishing characteristic of a Freemason's heart, namely Charity,' in the abstract; and the Charity Representative would follow with such moderate detail of the results of the beneficence of the Craft as will interest and not weary his hearers.

This subject has been here somewhat fully discussed, because Charity being, as it were, the watchword of our Order, the younger brethren, learning that it is no unmeaning cry, no 'sounding brass or tinkling cymbal,' but a substantial reality among us ; that we do minister to the relief of ' our poor and distressed brethren, and their widows, and their helpless orphan children ;' that all is done without degrading the recipients, and without wounding their self-respect ; that, judged by results, our Charities are the best managed and the most successful organizations in existence ; that, with scarcely an exception, the scholars who have passed through the Boys' and the Girls' Schools respectively have done credit to the Institutions, and in some instances have achieved eminent success in their after-life ; and that the closing years of life are rendered comfortable and happy for many an aged brother, and many an otherwise unprovided for and hopeless widow. Having the knowledge of these good works of our Order imparted by ' one who knows,' ' the best feelings of the heart may be awakened to acts of Beneficence and Charity,' to the lasting advantage of our Charitable Institutions, and to the realization on the part of the givers of the fact that in very deed ' It is more blessed to give than to receive.'

There may be other occasions, such as the presence of a visitor of distinction, or the presentation of an address, or a testimonial (a jewel—or something of the kind), as an acknowledgment of eminent services rendered to the Lodge, when something more than a hasty and perhaps ill-considered address is required of the speaker. A very nice discrimination is necessary in treating these subjects ; the speaker is required to avoid, on the one hand, excessive laudation, manifestly beyond the merits of the recipient, and on the other hand, the equally manifest falling short in the expression of appreciation of those merits, and in giving utterance to the sentiments of those of whom he is the mouthpiece.

A difficult task, generally, is that of replying to the toast of one's own health, or of expressing one's grateful feelings as the recipient of the testimonial mentioned, whatever form it may take. There is always the initial difficulty of having one's self as the topic upon which to dilate. We cannot take others into our full confidence as to our opinion of ourselves. We can but follow, to a limited extent, 'the remarks of the brother who has done us the honour of,' etc., etc.; 'We can but deprecate the too eulogistic remarks which he has uttered, the high encomiums he has passed upon us, the panegyrics, approaching, if not reaching, the region of hyperbole so infinitely beyond our merits,' etc., etc.

This is the sort of thing one hears, not often expressed in absurdly inflated language such as that given in the preceding paragraph, but the same in kind, differing only in degree. The truth of the matter is, we should never cease to be natural in our utterances; the tongue should speak that which the heart dictates, and if our utterances bear the stamp of truthfulness, if they have the ring of the true metal, be they the utterances of a novice or the well-rounded periods of a practised speaker, they will not fail of their full effect upon the hearers.

On April 16th, in the year 1890, the following appeared in the Paris news column of one of the London papers (M. Floquet was addressing the Freemasons of Bordeaux) : 'In conclusion, M.

13

Floquet appealed in eloquent language to "the Principles of Liberty, Equality, and Fraternity, which were the Principles of Freemasonry."' The author of this work was present at the Initiation of the late Canon Portal, one of the best known and distinguished Brothers of our Order during the last fifty years. At the banquet Brother Portal replied to the toast of the newly-initiated Brethren ; he made a short but admirably expressed speech, with a peroration which ran thus : ' ... he had found in Freemasonry that which the world had long been looking for in vain : true Liberty, Equality, and Fraternity.' Truly history repeats itself.

Brother George Raymond Portal had already gained distinction in 'The Union' as a ready and fluent debater ; no one was astonished to hear from him a speech so far above the average of the utterances of Entered Apprentices, in reply to the toast of their health.

CHAPTER XXIII

Duty of D. of C. to Marshal all Processions, etc.—The Check
upon too frequent Public Demonstrations—How the Dispensation is to be obtained—Order of a Procession—Order
reversed at the Appointed Place—If the Occasion be laying
a Foundation, or Chief Corner Stone—If the Edifice to be
erected be a Church—An Interesting Feature—An Instance
of laying a Chief Corner Stone—An Instance of the Consecration of a Lodge—Customs vary in different Provinces—
Where to apply in Doubt or Difficulty—Who controls the
Proceedings—A Masonic Funeral—Widely divergent Opinions
on the Practice—In one Province it was sought to be inter-
dicted—Much may be said on both Sides—But the Older
Members especially regard it with Reverence—Its Impressiveness and Solemnity—Three typical Masonic Funerals described
from Personal Experience—Must have been the Wish of the
Deceased Brother—'The last sad Office of Respect'—The
Power of Veto always with the Authorities—Mode of addressing written Communications to those in Authority.

ONE important duty attached to the Office of Director
of Ceremonies, is 'to marshal all processions and
demonstrations of the Brethren.' We may remark
in connection with this subject that a rule exists
which gives to the Rulers of the Order the power to
put a check upon the—possibly otherwise—too frequent public demonstrations of the Brethren. Rule
No. 206 of the Book of Constitutions expressly states
that no Brother shall appear in Masonic clothing in

public without a dispensation from the Grand Master or the Provincial or District Grand Master.

As a matter of course, the petition for a Dispensation would set forth fully and clearly the object of the demonstration. The petition would necessarily be sent to the Grand Secretary, or in the Provinces or Districts to the Provincial or District Grand Secretary, as indeed etiquette demands that all written communications to the high dignitaries mentioned should invariably be so sent.

One general rule would appear to apply to the marshalling of all processions of our Order, some details being occasionally superadded to suit the varying purposes of the demonstration. The Tyler with a drawn sword heads the procession; next follow Entered Apprentices two and two; then Fellow-Crafts, followed by the Master Masons, juniors leading; next the Assistant Officers of the Lodge, the lowest first; then Past Masters, juniors first; next the Immediate Past Master; the Banner of the Lodge; the Worshipful Master, supported on the right by the Senior Warden, and on the left by the Junior Warden, each of the Wardens carrying his Column. After these come Provincial or District Grand Officers, the lower in rank going first, Grand Officers bringing up the rear; among the Provincial, or District, or Grand Officers, being probably the one appointed to perform the Ceremony, if any. He would be in the last rank, supported on each side by Brethren of distinction and of high rank in the Craft.

It is necessary that all (except those mentioned as being supported right and left) should form *two deep*, as will be seen in the next sentence. On arriving at the appointed place, the Tyler halts, and the whole of the Brethren, down to but not including the rear rank, separate and form two lines. Those in the rear rank walk forward between the lines, and each two of the Brethren as they are reached fall in behind, and so on, until the whole order of the procession is inverted, and those—the juniors—who were first, become the last.

If the occasion be the laying of a foundation, or Chief Corner Stone, the requisite number of distinguished Brethren are appointed to bear the Square, the Level, and the Plumb-rule, the Heavy Mall, and the Trowel, the Corn, the Wine, and the Oil. Others carry the bottle containing the coins, etc., the brass plate with the inscription, and whatever else it may be thought necessary to carry in the procession. The Architect carries the plans of the building.

If the edifice to be erected be a Church or Church Schools, the open Bible with the Square and Compasses is carried frequently by the Tyler. A board of the necessary size, covered probably with crimson velvet or cloth, with a cushion upon it, would be provided. Two broad straps or ribbons passed over the Tyler's shoulders would enable him to carry the whole with perfect ease, and he would have his right hand free to carry the sword.

On one occasion when the writer was present the open Bible was carried upon a board made for the purpose, having four handles extending horizontally, two in front, and two at the back. The bearers were four little boys, *each boy a Lewis*. Nothing in the whole procession attracted so much interest as those four little bearers of the Bible, all apparently under ten years of age. The Deputy Provincial Grand Master who laid the Chief Corner Stone, afterwards sent an enduring memento of the occasion to each of the boys. It would be interesting to know if they — or any of them — eventually became Free-masons.

During the time when the writer was Master of a Lodge in the far west of England, the Members of his Lodge erected a Masonic Hall. The Chief Corner Stone was laid by the Deputy Provincial Grand Master, assisted by a number of Provincial Grand Officers. One of these of high rank regulated the whole pro-ceedings. On that occasion the Tracing Board of the First Degree, on a light frame with four handles — an enlarged edition of that mentioned in the preceding paragraph — ornamented white and gold, was carried by four Past Masters of the Lodge. This Tracing Board was supposed to represent the Lodge in a symbolic sense.

It would probably have been more correct to have had the three Tracing Boards. At the Consecration of a Lodge in a large public building—not the Lodge-room—at which the writer was present, the three Tracing Boards, piled (horizontally) one upon another, were placed upon a stand in the centre of the hall, presumably representing the Lodge. A very Worship-ful Brother, high in Office in Grand Lodge, was the presiding Officer; the Wardens were also very Worship-ful Members of Grand Lodge, and the then Grand Director of Ceremonies assisted, so no doubt can be entertained of the strictly correct manner in which everything was carried out.

Customs, however, vary in different Provinces, and a practice which is held to be strictly correct in one Province would be utterly condemned in another. In all cases of Public Ceremonial, if any doubt or difficulty should arise, application should be made to the Grand or Provincial, or District Grand Secretary, according to locality, for counsel and guidance.

When the chief Functionary is the Provincial, or District Grand Master, or his Deputy, or any of his past or present Officers specially appointed to officiate in his stead, the Provincial, or District Grand Secretary, would, as a rule, take the control of the proceedings, assisted, of course, by the Officers of the Lodge, or Lodges, chiefly interested in the Ceremony to be performed. In the case of the Grand Master himself, or the Pro-Grand Master, or the Deputy Grand Master, or other high Officer of Grand Lodge officiating, the Grand Secretary would dictate the course of the proceedings, and would give his instructions to the Brethren who, under him, would have the charge of the preparations.

One other occasion for a 'public procession of Freemasons clothed with the Badges of the Order' is a Masonic funeral. Widely divergent opinions will be found to exist in different Provinces, and even in different portions of the same Province, as to the desirability, or otherwise, of continuing the practice of this undoubtedly ancient custom in the Craft. In some Provinces it may be considered obsolete, or is possibly almost, or altogether unknown.

In one Province, well known to the writer, where the custom of burying with Masonic Ceremonial was rather frequently practised, a feeling adverse to the custom was known to exist on the part of some two or three Provincial Grand Officers (not the highest in authority), and an attempt was made to pass a resolution in Provincial Grand Lodge interdicting the practice in that province; the motion, however, was negatived by a substantial majority, chiefly representatives of Lodges favourable to its continuance.

Very much may be said upon both sides of the question. Of its lawfulness there is no doubt whatever; it is upon its expediency that the doubt may arise. As supplementary to the comprehensive and beautiful Burial Service of the Church of England, the tacking on of our Masonic Service at the end appears to many to be a supererogatory proceeding; to some an anti-climax. Many, on the other hand, especially older members of the Craft, regard it with an extreme reverence, and believe in its impressiveness and solemnity, and in its possibly lasting good effect upon the hearers.

Three cases drawn from memory may here be cited. A Nonconformist Brother, a zealous Freemason, and an old Past Master, had—on his deathbed (a necessary condition)—expressed the desire to be buried with Masonic Ceremonial. A programme of the full Ceremony was furnished, a few days previously to the funeral, to the minister who was to officiate on the occasion. He, the minister, being bound by no rule or Ritual, so composed and arranged his portion of the service, as to lead up to and to fit in with the Masonic Ceremony. The result was that all went admirably and harmoniously as two component parts of one perfect whole. There was no incongruity, no superfluity.

The second case was that of the oldest Past Master, in the district in which he had spent a long and active life; he had been highly distinguished in Freemasonry for many years, and had borne high office in Provincial Grand Lodge. He had a long lingering illness, the fatal result of which he never doubted. He repeated his wish again and again, that his obsequies should be performed with Masonic Rites. The reading of the lengthy address in the Masonic Ceremony is really the duty of the Worshipful Master of the Lodge, of which the deceased had been a member; but on this occasion, by the often expressed desire of the deceased Brother, the author of these pages as his closest friend read that address. All this would be scarcely worth relating, but for that which follows.

The interment took place in a country churchyard, near to the birth-place of the deceased. The Vicar (who had been made fully aware that some Masonic Ceremonial would be performed), immediately upon the conclusion of the Burial Service of the Church, took his departure, without a word, and remained in the vestry until those concerned went in to pay the fees, after the conclusion of the Masonic Ceremony. Very many present, including a number of non-Freemasons, considered that the Vicar had shown a bigoted and intolerant spirit. It is possible, however, that he acted in accordance with his conscientious convictions; he probably felt that a service, not sanctioned by the

Church, should not be performed upon ground conse-
crated by the Church. Such a view may be narrow;
but if it be conscientiously held, it is entitled to
respect.

The third instance was the interment of the remains
of a Provincial Grand Master—a man of mark in his
county, a territorial magnate, and a zealous Freemason. A very large gathering of the Brethren, of
the deceased's own, and of the neighbouring Province,
assembled, including the majority of the then present
and past Provincial Grand Officers. A choir—Freemasons, with some female voices—had been provided.
Two, at least, of the sons of the deceased, who were
Freemasons, were 'clothed with the Badges of the
Order.' The aged widow sat by the grave-side. The
Burial Services of the Church and that of our Order
were admirably rendered—there appeared no want of
harmony between them; the effect of the whole was
solemn and impressive in a high degree. The clergy
remained throughout, up to the end. The eldest son
became, and is now, Grand Master of his Province,
and a Warden in Grand Lodge.

One could not help calling to mind the lines:

'The widow's and the orphans' tears bedewed the cold grave-
side
Of that fine old English gentleman.'

The foregoing—all personal experiences—have been
given here in order to show that the advocates for the
retention of the custom in question are not without
precedents, supplying good arguments in favour of
their views: that the practice — if it be at all an

anachronism—is not obsolete; that men of high degree, as well as those of a lower grade, continue to express the wish, that the Brethren with whom they have been associated in life should join with their immediate connections in 'performing the last sad office of respect' to their remains.

The fact, also (previously mentioned), should not be lost sight of, that no such Ceremony, nor, indeed, any demonstration of Freemasons (in clothing), can take place without the permission of the Grand Master, or of those to whom he may delegate the authority to grant dispensations for such public occasions. The power of veto therefore always rests with the authorities, and we may presume that in every case good cause must be shown for the application, or it would not be granted. (See Appendix N, page 273.)

We may here mention briefly the mode of addressing any written communication to those in authority over us. No one would be so presumptuous as to address H.R.H. the Grand Master, except in the form of a petition, which would be forwarded to the Grand Secretary. The heading of such a petition will be found in Article 119 of the Book of Constitutions. The Pro-Grand Master is entitled to the prefix Most Worshipful, in virtue of his Office as the immediate representative of the Grand Master. The Deputy-Grand Master, and all Provincial and District Grand Masters, are entitled Right Worshipful. Deputy-Provincial Grand Masters, and the higher Officers of Grand Lodge, including the Grand Secretary and the Grand Registrar, are Very Worshipful. The Master of a Lodge, as every Freemason knows, is entitled

Worshipful. Whether it be in oral or written addresses, the several titles should always be strictly observed. We venture, however, again to caution Brethren that all written communications to the higher authorities should always pass through the hands of the Grand, or Provincial, or District Grand Secretary; and, even then, that Brethren should not address those high Officers without good and sufficient reason.

Some remarks upon the Ceremony of the Installation of a Worshipful Master will be found in the Appendix L, p. 264.

CHAPTER XXIV.

THE first pages of this work set forth clearly its object and intentions. In accordance with the indication there given of the scope of our inquiry into, and discussion of, the subject of 'the Etiquette of Freemasonry,' the early chapters, more or less discursive in their character, were devoted to the consideration of 'duties and details,' 'means and appliances,' 'technicalities and ceremonial observances—as distinct from the verbal portions of the Ceremonies—which are indispensably necessary for the decorous and harmonious working of the business of the Lodge.'

Having fully considered every subject which can be included under those several heads, some chapters were devoted to the discussion of various portions of the several Ceremonies of the three Degrees, including, in our view, not only action and position, but occasionally venturing to insert—for the sake of clearness in explanation—certain portions of the Ritual itself. Then, 'calling from labour to refreshment,' we devoted some chapters to the Etiquette of the Table.

Under this latter head no mention was made of the first of the four Cardinal Virtues—Temperance. This omission was wittingly made. A homily upon this virtue, addressed to the Members of our Order, would be an impertinence. Our Banquets and Festivals, and the more ordinary monthly hours of relaxation and refreshment, are conducted with a degree of order and propriety, and of regard for temperance in the use of 'creature comforts,' which are not merely creditable to ourselves, but may be said to be in strict accordance with the spirit of Freemasonry.

Men—like the writer—of the older generation could not but be aware of occasional deviations from the strict observance of temperance on the part of some Members of our Order. At that time it was not thought to be disgraceful for men in a good position in society to occasionally, or even frequently, exceed the bounds of sobriety—even the coarse expression, 'as drunk as a lord,' might have had some slight foundation for its origin and common use. At the time mentioned, there is no doubt that, in some of our Lodges, certain Brethren did, by late hours and by excess at the monthly meetings, bring the Craft into considerable disrepute; and occasioned, on the part of many wives and mothers, a strong prejudice against Freemasonry, and in very many cases a serious objection to their husbands or their sons becoming Freemasons.

Happily, the prejudice, and the cause of it, are now things of the past. We have even total abstinence Lodges on the Register of Grand Lodge. The author was present at the Consecration of one of these, the 'Wolseley Lodge,' named after Lord Wolseley, who attended the Consecration. Either in his speech, or in conversation at the banquet, he disclaimed for himself the character of a total abstainer; he was a votary of temperance, but in his campaigns of Coomassie and the Soudan he had strongly recommended to his men total abstinence ; and as an example, as well as from his conviction of its efficacy in hot climates, he had practised it himself.

The later chapters of our work are devoted to some remarks upon 'public processions and demonstrations,' and to the consideration of the several occasions which are the causes of these processions, etc. The last of these occasions which we have specified is the Masonic Ceremonial at the funeral of a deceased Brother. Having thus arrived at 'the brink of the grave . . . which, when this transitory life shall have passed away, will receive us into its cold bosom,' 'nothing now remains but' to say farewell, with 'hearty good wishes' to every Brother who shall have read these pages to the end.

THE PROVINCIAL OR DISTRICT GRAND LODGE.

Custom of being invited by the Different Lodges—Arrangements for holding Provincial or District Grand Lodge—Three
subsidiary Rooms required—Opening the Lodge visited—
Marshalling the Procession—Order of Entering the Lodge—
Ceremonies of Opening and Closing Provincial or District
Grand Lodge—Variation for Grand Lodge—Mode of addressing Deputy Provincial or District G. M.

IN many Provinces and Districts the Provincial or
District Grand Lodge is invited by the different
Lodges to hold its meetings one year in one locality
and another year in another. In some Provinces two
meetings are held in the year. The Lodge which is
honoured by a visit is expected to make—under the
direction of the Provincial Grand Secretary, assisted
by the P. G. Director of Ceremonies—all arrangements
for the proper reception and accommodation of the
Provincial or District Grand Lodge, and for the
Members of the various Lodges. The meetings
being as a rule larger than could be accommodated in
an ordinary Lodge-room, a room is engaged in some
large building, sufficiently capacious for the general
meeting, and some other rooms (preferably in the
same building), one for the reception of the Provincial
or District Grand Master (who requires a room for
his exclusive use) ; another for Provincial or District
Grand Officers, and a third for the Brethren generally.

The Brethren, not having present or past Provincial or District rank, enter the Lodge room. The Worshipful Master and the Wardens of the Lodge visited occupy the three chairs, and open the Lodge in the three Degrees.

The Provincial Grand Director of Ceremonies marshals the Provincial or District Grand Officers in processional order, the Provincial or District Grand Master at the rear. Arrived at the door of the Lodge the report is given, the Provincial or District Grand Officers open out right and left, the Provincial or District Grand Master walks up the centre, the Senior Officers closing in ; the others do the same, and in that inverted order they enter the Lodge. The Brethren all rise, and the Organist plays a march, or some appropriate composition, while the Provincial or District Grand Master and the Officers take their seats.

The Master of the Lodge and the Wardens back out of their respective places and hand in their Provincial or District successors. The Provincial or District Grand Lodge is then opened in the following form :

The Ceremony of Opening a Provincial or District Grand Lodge.

(*We will use the initials of a Provincial Grand Master with the prefix of R. W. for Right Worshipful. A District Grand Master is also Right Worshipful. The Ceremony of opening Grand Lodge is precisely the same as the following, with the full title Most Worshipful Grand Master. If a Deputy Provincial or*

Deputy District Grand Master should preside, he would be addressed as Very Worshipful, etc.)

R. W. P. G. M.—(━━┳) Brethren, assist me to open this Provincial Grand Lodge. (*All rise.*)

R. W. P. G. M.—Bro. Provincial Grand Pursuivant, where is your situation in Provincial Grand Lodge?

P. G. P.—Within the Inner Porch of Provincial Grand Lodge, Right Worshipful Provincial Grand Master.

R. W. P. G. M.—What is your duty?

P. G. P.—To give a proper report of all approaching Brethren, and to see that they are properly clothed and are ranged under their respective banners.

R. W. P. G. M.—Do you find them so ranged?

P. G. P.—I do, Right Worshipful Provincial Grand Master, to the best of my knowledge.

R. W. P. G. M.—Where is the situation of the Provincial Junior Grand Warden?

P. G. P.—In the South, Right Worshipful Provincial Grand Master.

R. W. P. G. M.—Bro. Provincial Junior Grand Warden, whom do you represent?

P. J. G. W.—..., the Prince of the people on Mount Tabor.

R. W. P. G. M.—Bro. Provincial Junior Grand Warden, where is the situation of the Provincial Senior Grand Warden?

P. J. G. W.—In the West, Right Worshipful Provincial Grand Master.

R. W. P. G. M.—Bro. Provincial Senior Grand Warden, whom do you represent?

P. S. G. W.—..., the Assistant High Priest on Mount Sinai.

R. W. P. G. M.—Bro. Provincial Senior Grand Warden, where is the situation of the Deputy Provincial Grand Master?

P. S. G. W.—At the right of the Right Worshipful Provincial Grand Master.

R. W. P. G. M.—Bro. Deputy Provincial Grand Master, whom do you represent?

D. P. G. M.—H. A. B., the Prince of Architects.

R. W. P. G. M.—What is your duty?

D. P. G. M.—To lay lines, to draw designs, and to assist the Right Worshipful Provincial Grand Master in carrying on the work.

R. W. P. G. M.—Very Worshipful Deputy Provincial Grand Master, where is the situation of the Provincial Grand Master?

D. P. G. M.—In the East.

R. W. P. G. M.—Whom does he represent?

D. P. G. M.—The Royal Solomon.

R. W. P. G. M.—Worshipful Bro. Chaplain, you will invoke the blessing of T. G. A. O. T. U. To order, Brethren.

(*The Prayer by the Chaplain.*)

R. W. P. G. M.—Brethren, in the name of the Royal Solomon, whose representative I am,* I declare

---

* Here the Provincial Grand Master very fitly and appropriately speaks in 'the name of the Royal Solomon,' because he is his 'representative.' The Master of a Lodge cannot claim to be the representative of the Almighty, and he has therefore not the least right to speak in His name at any time, nor has the Senior Warden for the same reason.

this Provincial Grand Lodge opened in ample form. (━▮ *Followed by the Wardens, the Provincial Grand Pursuivant, and the Tyler.*)

P. G. D. of C.—Brethren, I call upon you to salute the Provincial Grand Master with the Gr. and R...l S...n seven times—thus.

This is done by all present, including Provincial Grand Officers.

P. G. D. of C.—Brethren, I call upon you to salute the Deputy Provincial Grand Master with the Gr. and R...l S...n five times—thus.

(*This is done by all present; then the Provincial Grand Officers sit down.*)

P. G. D. of C.—Brethren, I call upon you to salute the Provincial Grand Officers past and present, with the Gr. and R...l S...n three times—thus. (*Done.*)   Brethren, be seated.

Closing Provincial or District Grand Lodge.

P. G. M.—(━▮) Brethren, assist me to close this Provincial Grand Lodge.   (*All rise.*)

P. G. M.—Brother Provincial Grand Pursuivant, you will prove the Provincial Grand Lodge close tyled.   (*This is done.*)

P. G. P.—Right Worshipful Provincial Grand Master, the Provincial Grand Lodge is close tyled.

P. G. M.—Worshipful Brother Chaplain, you will render thanksgivings to the Most High for all His mercies.—To order, Brethren.

(*Prayer and Praise by the Chaplain.*)

P. G. M.—Brethren, in the name of the Royal Solomon, whose representative I am, I declare this Provincial Grand Lodge closed. (*Gives the k...s of the M. M. Degree.*)

(*The Provincial Grand Master, followed by his Officers present and past, leaves the Lodge, the Brethren all standing, and the Organist performing his duty.*

(*The Worshipful Master, and the Officers, resume their several places, and the Craft Lodge is closed in three Degrees.*)

THE CEREMONY OF LAYING A FOUNDA-
TION, OR CHIEF CORNER STONE.

Opening the Lodge—Arrangement of the Procession—Form of
Address—Ceremony of Laying the Stone—Return of the
Procession.

As a rule, some high dignitary of the Craft lays the
stone. In this copy of the Ceremony the title of
Provincial Grand Master will be used.

A Craft Lodge is opened in a convenient room,
and there the procession is formed; the Provincial
Grand Director of Ceremonies, assisted by the local
D. C., arranging the Brethren in the proper order.
See page 197.

The Provincial Grand Master having arrived at his
station, a flourish of trumpets is given, or a hymn or
an ode is sung, or music is played, as may have been
arranged.

The Provincial Grand Master delivers an address,
either composed to suit the occasion, or in general
terms as follows:

PROVINCIAL GRAND MASTER'S ADDRESS.

Men and Brethren, here assembled to behold this
Ceremony. Be it known unto you, that we be true
and lawful Freemasons, the successors of those
ancient Brethren of our Craft, who from time im-

memorial have been engaged throughout the civilized world in 'the erection of stately and superb edifices,' to the glory of God, and for the service of mankind. From those ancient Brethren have been handed down from generation to generation certain secrets 'by which Freemasons are known to each other, and are distinguished from the rest of the world.' Those secrets are lawful, and honourable, and 'are in no way incompatible with our moral, our civil, or our religious duties'; and as we have received them from our predecessors in the Order, so we hand them down pure and unimpaired to those who are to succeed us.

Our Order has always been distinguished for loyalty to the Throne, for obedience to the laws and institutions of the country in which we reside, for good citizenship, for goodwill to all mankind, and especially for 'that most excellent gift—Charity!' By the exercise of these qualities we have in all ages enjoyed such distinction, that princes and nobles of high degree have been Members of our Order, 'have patronised our mysteries, and have joined in our assemblies.' Under such powerful protection, and by the fidelity and zeal of its Members, Freemasonry has endured through the ages, and has been enabled 'to survive the wreck of mighty empires, and to resist the destroying hand of time.'

We have met here to-day, in the presence of this great assembly, to lay the Chief Corner Stone of this building, which is about to be erected to the honour and glory of the Most High, and in humble dependence upon His blessing.

As Freemasons, our first and paramount duty in all our undertakings is, to invoke the blessing from T. G. A. O. T. U. upon that which we are about to do; I therefore call upon you to give attention to the Provincial Grand Chaplain, and to unite in prayer to Him from Whom alone cometh every good and every perfect gift.

(*The stone will now be raised.*)

(*Prayer by the Provincial Grand Chaplain.*)

Chant (*omnes*).—So mote it be.

P. G. M.—I now declare it to be my will and pleasure that the Chief Corner Stone of this building be laid. Brother Provincial Grand Secretary, you will read the inscription on the plate. (*Which is done.*)

(*The stone will be lowered about nine inches: during the process of lowering the Choir will sing the first verse of ' Prosper the Art.'*)

SOLO.

When the Temple's first stone was slowly descending,
    A stillness like death the scene reigned around ;
There thousands of gazers in silence were bending,
    Till rested the ponderous mass on the ground.

CHORUS.

Then shouts filled the air and the joy was like madness,
    The Founder alone, standing meekly apart ;
Until from his lips burst—flowing with gladness,
    The wish that for ever might prosper the Art.

P. G. M.—Brother Provincial Grand Treasurer you will deposit the vessel containing the coins and other articles in the cavity.

(The Bottle containing the Parchment, with an account of the undertaking, and the names of the principal personages taking part in the Ceremony, various current coins of the Realm, and copies of local papers, will be placed in the cavity. The cavity should now be filled with powdered charcoal. The plate will then be cemented in its place over all.)

*(The Stone is again lowered nine inches, during which the Choir will sing the second verse of '*Prosper the Art.*')*

SOLO.

When the Temple had reared its magnificent crest,
  And the wealth of the world had embellished its
    walls,
The nations drew near from the East and the West,
  Their homage to pay in its beautiful halls.

CHORUS.

Then they paused at the entrance, with feelings
    delighted,
  Bestowing fond looks ere they turned to depart ;
And as homeward they journeyed with voices united,
  They joined in full chorus, with 'Prosper the Art.'

(The trowel is presented with some appropriate remarks, and the Provincial Grand Master spreads the cement.)

*(Solemn music may be played, or the '*Gloria*' may be sung, while the Stone is lowered into its place.)*

P. G. M.—Brother Junior Warden, what is the Emblem of your Office ?

J. W.—The Plumb-rule, Right Worshipful Provincial Grand Master.

P. G. M.—How do you apply the Plumb-rule?

J. W.—To adjust and prove all uprights, while fixing them upon their proper bases.

P. G. M.—Brother Junior Warden, you will apply the Plumb-rule to the sides of the Stone. (*This is done.*)

J. W.—Right Worshipful Provincial Grand Master, I find the Stone to be perfect and trustworthy.

P. G. M.—Brother Senior Warden, what is the Emblem of your Office?

S. W.—The Level, Right Worshipful Provincial Grand Master.

P. G. M.—How do you apply the Level?

S. W.—To lay levels and to prove horizontals.

P. G. M.—Brother Senior Warden, you will prove the Stone. (*Done.*)

S. W.—Right Worshipful Provincial Grand Master, I find the Stone to be level and well founded.

P. G. M.—Worshipful Master, what is the Emblem of your Office?

W. M.—The Square, Right Worshipful Provincial Grand Master.

P. G. M.—How do you apply the Square?

W. M.—To try and adjust all rectangular corners of buildings, and to assist in bringing rude matter into due form.

P. G. M.—You will apply the Square. (*This is done.*)

W. M.—Right Worshipful Provincial Grand Master, I have applied the Square, and I find the Stone to be well wrought and true.

(The Provincial Grand Master himself applies the Plumb-rule, the Level, and the Square.)

P. G. M.—I find the Stone to be plumb, level, and square, and that the Craftsmen have laboured skilfully.

(The mallet is presented to the P. G. M. with some appropriate remarks.)

(The P. G. M. gives three knocks on the Stone with the mallet.)

P. G. M.—May T. G. A. O. T. U. look down with favour upon this undertaking, and may He crown the edifice of which we have laid the foundation with abundant success.

(Flourish of Trumpets, or Music, or the Choir and the Assembly may sing the following Chant :)

CHAPLAIN.—'Except the Lord build the house : their labour is but lost that build it.

'Except the Lord keep the city : the watchman waketh but in vain.

'It is in vain that ye rise up early, and late take rest : for so He giveth His beloved sleep.

'If the foundations be destroyed : what can the righteous do ?

'Her foundations are upon the holy hills : the Lord loveth the gates of Zion more than all the dwellings of Jacob.

'That our sons may grow up as the young plants : and that our daughters may be as the polished corners of the temple.

'Happy is the people that is in such a case : yea, happy is that people whose God is the Lord.'

(The Provincial Grand Superintendent of Works, or the Architect, presents the plans.)

P. G. S. of W.—Right Worshipful Provincial Grand Master, it is my duty to present these Plans of the intended building, which have been duly approved.

(*The Provincial Grand Master inspects the Plans and returns them to the Architect.*)

P. G. M.—I place in your hands the Plans of the intended building, having full confidence in your skill as a Craftsman, and I desire that you will proceed without loss of time to the completion of the work, in conformity with the plans and designs now entrusted to you.

BEARER OF THE CORN.—Right Worshipful Provincial Grand Master, I present to you Corn, the sacred emblem of Plenty.

(*The P. G. M. strews Corn upon the Stone.*)

CHAPLAIN.—' There shall be a handful of corn in the earth upon the top of the mountains : the fruit thereof shall shake like Lebanon : and they of the city shall flourish like grass of the earth.' (*Psalm* lxxii. 16.)

BEARER OF THE WINE.—Right Worshipful Provincial Grand Master, I present to you Wine, the sacred emblem of Truth.

(*The P. G. M. pours Wine on the Stone.*)

CHAPLAIN.—' And for a drink-offering thou shalt offer the third part of a hin of wine, for a sweet savour unto the Lord.' (*Numbers* xxviii. 14.)

BEARER OF THE OIL. — Right Worshipful Provincial Grand Master, I present to you Oil, the sacred emblem of Charity.

(*The P. G. M. pours Oil upon the Stone.*)

CHAPLAIN.—' And thou shalt make it an oil of holy

ointment, an ointment compound after the art of the apothecary : it shall be a holy anointing oil.

'And thou shalt anoint the tabernacle of the congregation therewith, and the ark of the testimony' (*Exodus* xxx. 25, 26).

P. G. M. (*or Chaplain*).—May the All-bounteous Creator of the Universe shower down His choicest blessing upon this (*names the building*), and grant a full supply of the Corn of nourishment, the Wine of refreshment, and the Oil of joy.

Chant (*Omnes*).—So mote it be.

(*Anthem or Te Deum.*)

CHAPLAIN.—May the Glorious Majesty of the Lord our God be upon us ; prosper Thou the work of our hands upon us, yea, the work of our hands establish Thou it.

Chant (*Omnes*).—So mote it be.

(*The following Masonic Version of the National Anthem may be sung.*

> God save our gracious King,
> Long live our noble King,
>   God save the King.
> Grant him victorious,
> Happy and glorious,
> Long to reign over us,
>   *God save the King.*
>
> Hail ! mystic light Divine,
> Long may thy radiance shine,
>   O'er sea and land.

Wisdom in thee we find,
Beauty and strength combined,
May we be ever joined
  In heart and hand.

Sing, then, ye Sons of Light,
In joyous strains unite,
    God save the King.
Long may King Edward reign,
Lord of the azure main,
Freemasons ! swell the strain,
    God save the King.

(*Procession, formed as before, returns to the place from
which it started.*)

THE CONSECRATION OF A LODGE.

A full and detailed Programme, with the Scripture Readings,
Dedicatory Ode, etc.

The Brethren assemble in the Lodge-room.

The Presiding Officer takes the Chair and appoints
his Officers *pro tem*.

The Lodge is opened in the Three Degrees.

HYMN.

Hail, Eternal ! by whose aid
All created things were made;
Heaven and earth Thy vast design ;
Hear us, Architect divine !

May our work, begun in Thee,
Ever blest with order be ;
And may we, when labours cease,
Part in harmony and peace.

By Thy glorious Majesty,
By the trust we place in Thee,
By the badge and mystic sign,
Hear us, Architect divine !
So mote it be.

The Presiding Officer addresses the Brethren on
the motive of the Meeting, and calls upon the
Chaplain to give the Prayer.

The D. C. addresses the Presiding Officer.

The Presiding Officer replies, and gives directions.

The Brethren of the New Lodge are ranged in order.

The **Prov. G. Sec.** reads the Petition and Warrant.

The Presiding Officer inquires of the Brethren if they approve of the Officers named in the Warrant.

The Brethren signify their approval in Masonic Form.

An Oration on the Nature and Principles of the Institution, by the Chaplain.

ANTHEM.

Behold how good and joyful a thing it is for Brethren
to dwell together in unity.

It is like the precious ointment upon the head, that
ran down unto the beard, even unto Aaron's
beard, and went down to the skirts of his clothing.

It is like the dew of Hermon which fell upon the hill
of Zion.

For there the Lord promised His blessing, and life for
evermore.   So mote it be.

Dedication Prayer.—First portion.

Chant (*Omnes*).—So mote it be.

All the Brethren turn towards the East while the Presiding Officer gives

THE INVOCATION.

Chant (*Omnes*).—So mote it be.

The Chaplain will read 2 Chron. ii. 1-16.

'And Solomon determined to build a house for the name of the Lord, and a house for His kingdom.

'And Solomon told out threescore and ten thousand men to bear burdens, and fourscore thousand to hew in the mountain, and three thousand and six hundred to oversee them.

'And Solomon sent to Huram the King of Tyre, saying, As thou didst deal with David my father, and didst send him cedars to build him a house to dwell therein, even so deal with me.

'Behold, I build a house to the name of the Lord my God, to dedicate it to Him, and to burn before Him sweet incense, and for the continual shewbread, and for the burnt-offerings morning and evening, on the Sabbaths, and on the new moons, and on the solemn feasts of the Lord our God. This is an ordinance for ever to Israel.

'And the house which I build is great : for great is our God above all gods.

'But who is able to build Him a house, seeing the heaven and heaven of heavens cannot contain Him ? who am I then, that I should build Him a house, save only to burn sacrifice before Him ?

'Send me now therefore a man cunning to work in gold, and in silver, and in brass, and in iron, and in purple, and crimson, and blue, and that can skill to grave with the cunning men that are with me in Judah and Jerusalem, whom David my father did provide.

'Send me also cedar trees, and algum trees, out of Lebanon ; for I know that thy servants can skill to cut timber in Lebanon ; and behold, my servants shall be with thy servants,

'Even to prepare me timber in abundance : for the house which I am about to build shall be wonderful great.

' And, behold, I will give to thy servants, the hewers that cut timber, twenty thousand measures of beaten wheat, and twenty thousand measures of barley, and twenty thousand baths of wine, and twenty thousand baths of oil.

' Then Huram the King of Tyre answered in writing, which he sent to Solomon, Because the Lord hath loved His people, He hath made thee king over them.

' Huram said, moreover, Blessed be the Lord God of Israel, that made heaven and earth, who hath given to David the king a wise son, endued with prudence and understanding, that might build a house for the Lord, and a house for His kingdom.

' And now I have sent a cunning man, endued with understanding, of Huram my father's,

' The son of a woman of the daughters of Dan, and his father was a man of Tyre, skilful to work in gold, and in silver, in brass, in iron, in stone, and in timber, in purple, in blue, and in fine linen, and in crimson ; also to grave any manner of graving, and to find out every device which shall be put to him, with thy cunning men, and with the cunning men of my lord David, thy father.

' Now therefore the wheat, and the barley, the oil, and the wine, which my lord hath spoken of, let him send unto his servants.

' And we will cut wood out of Lebanon, as much as thou shalt need : and we will bring it to thee in floats by sea to Joppa ; and thou shalt carry it up to Jeru-salem.'

The Lodge Board is then uncovered, and the Presiding Officer and Wardens carry the Elements of Consecration round the Lodge, halting in the East at each perambulation. (*Solemn music during the procession.*)

Before the first circuit the Brethren sing :

> When once of old, in Israel,
> Our early Brethren wrought with toil,
> Jehovah's blessings on them fell
> In showers of Corn, and Wine, and Oil.

When the first circuit is completed the Consecrating Officer strews Corn—the Emblem of Plenty.

Musical Response.—*Glory be to God on high.*

The Chaplain reads Psalm lxxii. 16.

'There shall be a handful of corn in the earth upon the top of the mountains ; the fruit thereof shall shake like Lebanon, and they of the city shall flourish like grass of the earth.'

Before the second circuit the Brethren sing :

> When there, a shrine to Him alone
> They built with worship sin to foil :
> On threshold and on corner-stone
> They poured out Corn, and Wine, and Oil.

When the second circuit is completed the Consecrating Officer pours Wine—the Emblem of Joy and Happiness.

Musical Response.—*Glory be to God on high.*

The Chaplain reads Nehemiah x. 39.

'For the children of Israel and the children of Levi shall bring the offering of the corn, of the new wine, and the oil, unto the chambers, where are the vessels of the sanctuary, and the priests that minister, and the porters, and the singers : and we will not forsake the house of our God.

Before the third circuit the Brethren sing :

> And we have come, fraternal bands,
>> With joy and pride, and prosperous spoil,
> To honour Him by votive hands
>> With streams of Corn, and Wine, and Oil.

When the third circuit is completed the Consecrating Officer pours Oil—the Emblem of Unity.

Musical Response.—*Glory be to God on high.*

The Chaplain reads Exodus xxx. 25, 26.

'And thou shalt make it an oil of holy ointment, an ointment after the art of the apothecary : it shall be a holy anointing oil.

'And thou shalt anoint the tabernacle of the congregation therewith, and the ark of the testimony.'

The Consecrating Officer alone perambulates the Lodge and sprinkles Salt—the Emblem of Friendship.

Musical Response.—*Glory be to God on high.*

The Chaplain reads Leviticus ii. 13.

' And every oblation of thy meat offering shalt thou season with salt ; neither shalt thou suffer the salt of the covenant of thy God to be lacking from thy meat offering : with all thine offerings thou shalt offer salt.'

THE PRESIDING OFFICER THEN DEDICATES THE LODGE.

ANTHEM.

'Holy, Holy, Holy, Lord God Almighty,
Heaven and earth are full of Thy glory.
Glory be to Thee O Lord most High.'

The Chaplain takes the Censer three times round
the Lodge and halts in the East.

Dedication Prayer.—Second portion.

Chant (*Omnes*).—So mote it be.

DEDICATORY ODE.*

Oh ! Thou *Architect* Eternal,
  Who of old Thy house didst bless,
Consecrate and fill this temple
  With Thy love and holiness.

Fill it with Thy heavenly *wisdom*,
  Let its walls in *strength* endure ;
Grace it with the inward *beauty*,
  That shall keep it ever pure.

Let the golden *Corn* of *plenty*,
  And of *joy* the sparkling *Wine*,
With the flowing *Oil* descending,
  Shed their influence benign.

Thus the *light* Thy presence lendeth,
  With a holy flame shall glow,
And each brother's heart enkindle,
  Love, *Relief*, and *Truth* to show.

* Specially written and composed by Brother Fred. J. W.
Crowe, S.D., and Organist, sung at the consecration of the
Ashburton Lodge, No. 2189, Ashburton, and now reprinted
here with Brother Crowe's kind permission.

THE PRESIDING OFFICER THEN CONSTITUTES THE LODGE.

Chant (*Omnes*).—So mote it be.

ANTHEM.

(*Dedication Prayer of King Solomon.*)

1. 'I have surely built Thee a house to dwell in, a settled place for Thee to abide for ever.'

2. 'But will God indeed dwell on the earth? Behold, the heaven and heaven of heavens cannot contain Thee ; how much less this house that I have builded ?'

3. 'Yet have Thou respect unto the prayer of Thy servant, O Lord my God, that Thine eyes may be open towards this house night and day, even toward the place of which Thou hast said, My name shall be there.

4. 'And the Lord said to Solomon, I have heard thy prayer. I have hallowed this house which thou hast built, to put my Name there for ever, and mine eyes and my heart shall be there perpetually. Hallelujah. Amen.' (1 Kings viii., ix.)

Final Benediction.

The Lodge is resumed in the Second Degree.

Installation of the Worshipful Master.

Election of Treasurer and Tyler.

Appointment and Investiture of Officers.

Election of Committee to frame By-laws.

Propositions for Initiation and Joining.

(See Appendix M, page 271.)

THE FUNERAL CEREMONY.

MASONIC RITUAL TO BE USED AT THE INTERMENT OF
A DECEASED BROTHER, WITH THE ADDRESSES, ETC.

*(To follow the usual funeral service of the religious
denomination to which the deceased brother belonged.)*

The Worshipful Master reads as follows :

Brethren.—The melancholy event which has
caused us to assemble on the present occasion cannot
have failed to impress itself on the mind of everyone
present. The loss of a friend and brother—especially
of one whose loss we now deplore—conveys a powerful
appeal to our hearts, reminding us as it does of the
uncertainty of life, and of the vanity of earthly hopes
and designs.

Amid the pleasures, the cares, and the various
avocations of life we are too apt to forget that upon
us also the common lot of all mankind must one day
fall, and that Death's dread summons may surprise us
even in the meridian of our lives, and in the full
spring-tide of enjoyment and success.

The ceremonial observances which we practise
during the obsequies of a departed Brother, are
intended to remind us of ' our own inevitable destiny,'
and to warn us that we also should be likewise ready,
for we know not the day nor the hour when in the

case of each of us 'the dust shall return to the earth as it was, and the spirit shall return unto God who gave it.'

Then, brethren, let us lay these things seriously to heart; let us strive in all things to act up to our Masonic profession, to live in accordance with the high moral precepts inculcated in our Ceremonies, and to practically illustrate in our lives and our actions the ancient tenets and established customs of the Order. Thus, in humble dependence upon the mercy of the Most High, we may hope, when this transitory life with all its cares and sorrows shall have passed away, to rejoin this our departed friend and brother in the Grand Lodge above, where the world's Great Architect lives and reigns supreme.

Chant (*omnes*).—So mote it be.

(*The following supplications are then offered by the Master:*)

MASTER.—May we be true and faithful, and may we live in fraternal affection one towards another, and die in peace with all mankind.

RESPONSE (*to be sung*).—So mote it be.

MASTER.—May we practise that which is wise and good, and always act in accordance with our Masonic profession.

RESPONSE (*to be sung*).—So mote it be.

MASTER.—May the Great Architect of the Universe bless us, and direct us in all that we undertake and do in His Holy Name.

RESPONSE (*to be sung*).—So mote it be.

(*The Secretary then advances and throws his roll into the grave, while the Master repeats, in an audible voice:*)

MASTER.—Glory be to God on high! on earth peace! good will towards men!

RESPONSE (*to be sung*).—So mote it be, now, henceforth, and for evermore!

There is a calm for those who weep,
    A rest for weary pilgrims found;
They softly lie and sweetly sleep,
    Low in the ground! low in the ground!

The storm that wracks the winter sky
    No more disturbs their deep repose,
Than summer evening's latest sigh,
    That shuts the rose! that shuts the rose!

Ah, mourner! long of storms the sport,
    Condemn'd in wretchedness to roam,
Hope thou shalt reach a sheltering port,
    A quiet home! a quiet home!

The sun is like a spark of fire,
    A transient meteor in the sky;
The soul, immortal as its sire,
    Shall never die! shall never die!

(*The Master then concludes the ceremony at the grave in the following words :*)

MASTER.—From time immemorial it has been the custom among the Fraternity of Free and Accepted Masons, at the request of a Brother on his death-bed, to accompany his corpse to the place of interment; and there to deposit his remains with the usual formalities of the Order. In conformity with this usage, and at the special request of our deceased brother, whose loss we deeply deplore, we are here assembled as Freemasons, to consign his body to the earth, and, openly before the world, to offer up in his memory the last tribute of our fraternal affection, thereby demonstrating the sincerity of our esteem for our deceased brother, and our inviolable attachment to the principles of the Order.

* [With all proper respect to the established customs of the country in which we live, with due deference to all in authority in Church and State, and with unlimited good-will to all mankind, we here appear as Freemasons, clothed with the insignia of the Order, and publicly express our submission to order and good government, and our wish to promote the general interests of mankind. Invested with ' the badge of innocence, and the bond of friendship,' we humbly bow to the Universal Parent, we implore His blessing on our zealous endeavours to promote peace and good-will, and we earnestly pray for His grace, to enable us to persevere in the *practice* of piety and virtue.]

The Great Creator having been pleased, in His infinite wisdom, to remove our worthy brother from the cares and troubles of this transitory life, and thereby to weaken the ties by which we are united to the world, may *we* who survive him, anticipating *our* own approaching end, be more strongly cemented in the bonds of union and friendship, and, during the short space which is allotted to us in our present existence, may we wisely and usefully employ our time

---

* The paragraph between the brackets [ ] may well be omitted ; it contains nothing appropriate to the occasion.

in the interchange of kind and fraternal acts, and may we strive earnestly to promote the welfare and happiness of our fellow men.

Unto the grave we have consigned the body of our deceased friend and brother, there to remain until the general resurrection, in the fullest confidence that both body and soul will then arise to partake of the joys which have been prepared for the righteous from the beginning of the world. And may Almighty God, of His infinite goodness, at that last grand tribunal, extend His mercy towards him, and all of *us*, and crown our hope with everlasting bliss, in the realms of a boundless eternity! This we beg, for the honour of His Name, to Whom be glory, now and for ever.

Chant (*omnes*).—So mote it be.

It is decreed in heaven above,
That we, from those whom best we love,
Must sever.
But hard the word would be to tell,
If to our friends we said farewell,
For ever.

And thus the meaning we explain—
We hope, and be our hope not vain,
That, though we part, we meet again.
A brief farewell; then meet again
For ever.

(See Appendix N, page 273.)

APPENDIX

A. —' The Revised Ritual of Craft Freemasonry.'
Extracts referred to.

A.—Extracts from 'The Revised Ritual of Craft Freemasonry' will be occasionally found in this work, and more especially in the Appendix. That the Ritual mentioned has some merit, may be judged by the extract from one of our Masonic publications contained in the advertisement at the end of this volume.

B.—The Tracing Boards.

First Tracing Board—Objections to the Second Tracing Board fully Considered—The Third Tracing Board.

B.—*Tracing Boards.*—Little needs to be remarked upon the Tracing Board of the First Degree. It is far from being all that can be desired, but it is not open to the strong objections which exist against the other two.

The objections to the second Tracing Board may be stated thus : The Explanation of the second Tracing Board, as given in the Rituals generally in use, is almost from the beginning to the end a series of statements having little or no foundation in fact ; and in several of its details it is diametrically opposed to the descriptions in the Bible of the things alluded to. There is no Scriptural warrant for the assertion that 'the Entered Apprentices received their wages in corn, wine, and oil, and the Fellow-Crafts theirs in money.' This, however, may be ranked among the *traditions*, and it is of small importance. In the Ritual it is stated that 'the Fellow-Crafts arrived at the middle chamber by way of a Porch, at the entrance of which stood two great Pillars.' This idea is partially embodied in the Tracing Board itself. There are depicted two columns under an arch, at the very entrance of the Temple, with a picturesque view of the open country, but *no Porch* at all. Almost from between the two columns springs a huge winding staircase, leading to a large and lofty vestibule, at the end of which is a doorway, with not a door, but a pair of curtains. The staircase clearly winds up to the *left side* of the building. The only description of the 'Chambers' is in 1 Kings vi. 5, 6 and 8. Verse 8 runs thus : 'The *door* for the middle chamber was in the *right side* of the house.' It is clear, therefore, that the staircase, so far from facing the very entrance of the Temple, was not seen at all until the door at 'the right side of the house' was opened; consequently, all that is said about the Porch and the Pillars applies to the main entrance to the Temple, and not in any sense to the middle chamber.

It is clearly stated in the Volume of the Sacred Law that the three chambers were 'built against the wall;' and they measured, respectively, five, six, and seven cubits, that is, about nine feet, ten feet nine inches, and twelve feet six inches in breadth (length not stated) ; therefore the Porch and the Pillars, etc., as applied to the middle chamber, are an absurdity. The two Pillars are asserted to have been made 'hollow, that they might serve as receptacles for the archives of Freemasonry.' Now, supposing such Records to have been then in existence, and to have been deposited in the two Pillars, how could they have been made accessible?—how arranged for reference? The thing is too absurd for argument. The Pillars were formed hollow then, as they would be now, because solid Pillars would have involved a vast waste of metal, and, from their enormous weight, such difficulty in moving and rearing, as would have taxed the skill of the Craftsmen to the uttermost. It is said 'they' (the Pillars) 'were further adorned with two spherical balls, on which were delineated maps of the Celestial and Terrestrial Globes.' In 1 Kings vii. 41, mention is made of 'the two *bowls* of the *chapiters*, that were on the top of the two pillars.' In verse 20 of the same chapter are these words, 'and the chapiters upon the two pillars had pomegranates also above, over against the *belly* which was by the network.' In these two extracts it would appear that '*bowl*' and '*belly*' both mean the swell of the capitals of the Pillars. These capitals were fixed at the tops of the shafts *in the usual way;* and the old compilers have here supposed that the *bowls* mentioned were identical with *spherical balls*, and those balls they have placed on the top of a square *above the chapiters*. The idea of these balls being covered with the delineations of the celestial and terrestrial Globes is sublime in its audacity. The first terrestrial Globe on record is that made by Anaximander of Miletus, B.C. 580, that

is considerably over *four hundred years* after the date
of the building of King Solomon's Temple; the
celestial Globe would probably be of even later date.
The height of the Pillars was each eighteen cubits,
and the chapiter five cubits, equal in the whole to
forty-one feet (one account, 2 Chronicles iii. 15, makes
them, the Pillar thirty-five cubits, and the chapiter
five cubits). Students of geography and astronomy
must have had some difficulty in consulting globes
placed at an elevation of from forty to fifty feet above
the ground. The assertion about these globes is as
wildly improbable as that the Pillars were 'formed
hollow that they might serve as receptacles for the
archives of Freemasonry.'

The remaining portion of the 'Explanation' needs
little comment. The account of the origin of the
P... W..., if narrated in the Lodge, should be given
(*or read*) in the very words of the Bible, rather than
in the commonplace phraseology of the old Rituals.
It should never have been printed. The winding staircase may or may not have comprised flights of three,
five, and seven steps. There is no mention of this
in the Bible. The Tracing Board shows fifteen continuous steps, without a break, or any indication of
these three flights. It is stated in the last clause of
the Explanation of the Tracing Board that 'when
they were *in the m... c...* their attention was particularly arrested by certain Hebrew characters.'
This is, of course, a pure invention. It is of little
moment, but it does not agree with the Tracing
Board, in which 'certain Hebrew characters' are
shown *above the doorway* at the end of the vestibule

and *outside* the m... c..., while in the centre, at the top of the Tracing Board, is a letter 'G' in a radiated triangle. The Tracing Board shows a strongly marked Mosaic Pavement, whereas in 1 Kings v. 30 it is clearly stated 'and the floor of the house he overlaid with gold within and without,' meaning, probably, the Temple proper, the Holy of Holies, and the Porch. *Not one word* indicating a Mosaic Pavement can be found in either of the two accounts of the building of the Temple.

The Porch and the Mosaic Pavement were evidently in high favour with the old compilers of the Ritual, They have both of these in their explanation of the Holy of Holies.

They have given their fancy very free play, and have paid but scant attention to the clear descriptions of the Temple in the Kings and the Chronicles. We should ask ourselves this question, Shall we follow the Bible ? or the vagaries (call them the 'teachings' if you will) of ill-informed and certainly careless compilers ? An allusion to the Tracing Board of the Third Degree will be found on page 149, also in the Appendix, C and D.

C AND D.—THE BURIAL OF H. A. B., ETC.

Intra-mural Interment expressly Forbidden by the Jewish Law —The Coffin not then in use—Only the Winding Sheet— White Aprons and Gloves.

C and D.— The following remarks embody all that needs to be said upon the subjects of the burial of H. A. B., and of the coffin, and incidentally of the Tracing Board of the Third Degree.

Perhaps the grossest absurdity of all in this connection is the statement 'he was not buried in the Holy of Holies, because nothing common or unclean,' etc. Evidently the old compiler considered it the height of *respectability* to be buried in the church, according to the bad old fashion existing in England some years ago, and he thought that H. A. B. would certainly be buried within the Temple, and he gives a reason (*in words borrowed from the New Testament*) why he was not buried in the Holy of Holies itself, being evidently ignorant of the fact that intra-mural interment was expressly forbidden by the Jewish Law. The Coffin is made a prominent object in this Degree. It is cited as one of the emblems of mortality, it is the most conspicuous (indeed almost the only conspicuous) thing on the older Tracing Boards. An actual coffin, sometimes in miniature, sometimes of full size, used to be (and in many places still is) brought into the Lodge, and actually used in the Third Degree. Many instances can be brought to prove that Coffins were not in use (then at least) in Judea. The Winding Sheet alone was used, and the body was carried on a Bier. In 2 Kings xiii. 21 it is related that a man was hastily cast into the ' sepulchre of Elisha, and when he touched the *bones* of Elisha, he revived and stood on his feet.' Now it is clear from this that neither the man nor Elisha could have been in a Coffin, and Elisha was one to whom all honour in burial would have been paid. In the Christian era clear proofs are found of the use solely of the Winding Sheet. Lazarus came forth out of the grave with the ' grave-clothes ' upon him. The

the Tracing Board. This Lecture consists chiefly of excerpts from the seven sections of the First Lecture.

In explaining the preparation of a Candidate for the Ceremony of Initiation, we will endeavour to adduce from Scripture, or from our own legendary lore, the origin and the intention of the various processes of that preparation. Briefly stated, as in the answer to one of the questions addressed to a Candidate for the Second Degree, the preparation for the Initiation is this. The Candidate is divested of all m... and h... w... d..., he has his r... a..., his l... b..., and l... k..., m... b..., and his r... h... s... s..., and has a c... t... about his n....

He is divested of all m... and m..., firstly, that he may bring nothing offensive or defensive into the Lodge to disturb its harmony; secondly, having been received into Freemasonry p... and p..., he should always thereafter be mindful of his duty to relieve indigent Brethren, as far as may be consistent with his own circumstances in life, and with the needs, and more especially with the merits, of the applicant; and thirdly, because at the erection of King Solomon's Temple 'there was no sound of a metal tool heard throughout the building.' We have this ' on proof of Holy Writ,' and our Traditions furnish us with the reason for this unprecedented course of proceeding. They tell us why all the materials, wood and stone, which had been prepared in the Lebanon, were put together at Jerusalem with wooden mauls and other non-metallic implements prepared expressly for the purpose—in these words: 'In the Vol. of the S. L. it is recorded that the Almighty spake unto Moses concerning an Altar, saying, "An Altar of earth shalt thou raise unto Me, whereon thou mayest offer thy sacrifices and thy burnt offerings ; but if thou wilt build it of stone, it shall be of unhewn stone, for if thou suffer a metal tool to pass upon it, thou wilt have polluted it, and no offering made thereon will be acceptable to Me." King Solomon, conceiving this Divine institution to be of force for all time, peremptorily forbade the use of metal tools in the construction of the Temple which he was about to erect, and to dedicate solely to the service of the Most High.' In accordance with this Divine precept, and following the pious example of King Solomon at the building of the Temple, we do not permit the Candidate to enter the Lodge with any metallic substance about him, except such as may necessarily belong to the articles of clothing which he may have upon him.*

The Candidate is h... w... firstly, that in the event of his refusal to go through any of the Ceremonies which are usual in the Initiation of a Freemason, he might be led out of the Lodge without discovering its form ; secondly, that his heart might conceive before his eyes were permitted to discover ; and thirdly, as he was admitted into Freemasonry in a s...

---

* Until within a comparatively recent period, a change of clothing, or the rough expedient of cutting off all metal buttons, was thought indispensable ; but in 1872 the then Grand Secretary, Bro. Hervey, wrote a letter, *with the personal approval of the Grand Master*, stating 'that in the present day the rule was to be taken to represent metals of value, money, or weapons.' It would be clearly impracticable to literally and absolutely carry out the words in question, as, if so, it would be necessary to remove the nails from the soles of *the boots*, and even the *stopping of a tooth.*

of d..., it should always remind him to keep all the world in d... with respect to our s..., except those who obtained them as lawfully as he was then about to do.

The r... a... of the Candidate is b...d, to show that he is able and ready to labour; his l... b... is made b..., so that nothing may be interposed between it and the p... of the P... extended thereto by the Inner Guard at the door of the Lodge ; and further, in order to certify beyond a doubt the sex of the Candidate. The l...k... is b...d, in accordance with the immemorial custom of the Order, which prescribes that the O...n of an Entered Apprentice shall always be taken upon the l... k... b... and bent.

The r... h... is s... s..., after an ancient custom derived from the East, the cradle of the human race and of Freemasonry, where a man 'plucked off his shoe' as a pledge of fidelity, and to render any solemn compact binding. A beautiful illustration of this ancient custom occurs in the Book of Ruth. It is of especial interest to Freemasons, on account of the name of one of the chief actors in this historical event being intimately connected with certain portions of our Ceremonies. You will remember that Boaz, the great-grandfather of David, desired to take to wife Ruth the Moabitess, the widow of Mahlon, the deceased son of Elimelech and Naomi. But he informed her that there was a certain man nearer of kin to Elimelech than himself, to whom the offer must first be made, to redeem the land that was Elimelech's, and with it to take Ruth to be his wife. This offer had to be made before competent witnesses. The manner in which this was done is related in the fourth chapter (see Ruth iv. 1-17).

An earlier allusion to the 'plucking off the shoe' will be found in Deuteronomy xxv. 7-10.

The earliest reference to the 'putting off the shoe' is in the Almighty's command to Moses on Mount Horeb, that he should put off his shoes from off his feet, because the ground whereon he stood was holy.

The Candidate has a c... t... about his n..., after a custom also derived from the East, where, in ancient times, men put r...s about the n... in token of humility and submission. An instance of this occurs in the First Book of Kings. The army of the Israelites under Ahab had defeated the army of the Syrians under Benhadad, 'and Benhadad fled and came into the city into an inner chamber' (1 Kings xx. 31-33).

This completes the preparation. Being thus d......d of l...t, and neither naked nor clothed, neither barefoot nor shod, but in a humble, halting, moving condition, the Candidate is led to the door of the Lodge.

F.—Poor Letter 'H.'

An Insoluble Mystery—The Malpractice to be found only in England—But not Confined to Cockneys—'Traps to Catch Cockneys'—Compensations in the Case—'The Enigma.'

F.—Why the letter *h* should be so frequently omitted in one place where it should be distinctly aspirated, and often thrust in where it should not be, is an insoluble mystery, and the more so seeing that the malpractice is found only in England. In Scotland and

Ireland, in Canada and in the United States of America, among all classes, from the highest to the lowest, the *h* is aspirated distinctly, whether it be at the beginning or the middle of a word. For instance, ' freehold ' and ' household ' with them are not ' free- 'old ' and ' ouse'old.' So with ' wheat ' and ' whisky '; no natives of those countries would omit the *h*. A braw Scot might say ' whusky,' he would not call it ' wusky.' In some of the London papers one sometimes sees, in repeating what an Irishman has said, the reporter gives ' fwat ' as the man's pronunciation of ' what,' which is nothing at all like it, the truth being that the reporter probably could not give the proper pronunciation of ' what ' to save his life. Many years ago —probably in a comic print, the following ' Traps to catch Cockneys ' appeared :

    ' The *horn* of the *hunter* is *heard* on the *hill ;*'

and

    ' The *heart* that is *humble* may *hope* for it *here,*

the *h* in humble being intended to be aspirated, as it now frequently is. Uriah Heep was always disgustingly ''umble,' and the readers of ' David Copperfield,' as a rule, at once restored the aspirate to the word. *Many clergymen do so.* And why not?

There is no reason why Cockneys should be especially held up to ridicule with regard to the letter *h*. Anyone who has resided for any period of time in different parts of England will have learned that with few exceptions,

    ' From Eddystone to Berwick Bounds,
    From Lynn to Milford Bay,'

among the working classes and those immediately above them—the lower-middle class—the misuse of the aspirate is so general as to be almost universal. Perhaps the greatest marvel of all is that in very many cases—perhaps the majority—the *h* omitted from its proper place is persistently brought in in another place where it has no right to be.

In Oxford (the very seat of learning), above all places, this habit is rampant. The writer used to hear, perhaps a dozen times a day, a tailor call out to his apprentice who worked in the top story, ''Enery, bring me a hiron.' Truly that 'hiron' entered into the soul of the hearer.

Among the poems '*attributed*' to Byron is the 'Enigma' on the letter *h*. It is worthy of being read, and even of being committed to memory, by all who would like to see the pure well of the English language kept undefiled. It runs thus:

''Twas w*h*ispered in *h*eaven, 'twas muttered in *h*ell,
And ec*h*o caught faintly the sound as it fell ;
On the confines of eart*h* 'twas permitted to rest,
And the dept*h*s of the ocean its presence confessed.
'Twill be found when the sp*h*eres shall be riven asunder,
'Tis seen in the lig*h*tning, 'tis heard in the t*h*under.
'Twas allotted to man with his earliest breat*h*,
It attends at his birt*h*, it awaits him in deat*h* ;
It presides o'er his *h*appiness, *h*onour, and *h*ealth,
'Tis the prop of his *h*ouse, 'tis the end of his wealt*h* ;
Without it the soldier or sailor may roam,
But woe to the wretch who expels it from *h*ome.
In the w*h*ispers of conscience its voice will he found,
Nor e'en in the w*h*irlwind of passion be drowned ;
'Twill not soften the *h*eart, but though deaf to the ear,
'Twill make it acutely and instantly *h*ear.
In s*h*ade let it rest, like a delicate flower—
Oh ! breathe on it softly—it dies in an *h*our.'

'The Enigma' sounds Byronic; the metre is the same as that of 'The Destruction of Sennacherib,' one of Byron's Hebrew melodies, and about which no doubt exists.

G.—The Charge in the First Degree.

A Marvellous Composition, well Adapted to its Purpose—Some Objections Considered—Explanations given for the Changes Introduced.

G.—The Charge in the First Degree, as it stands in some of the Rituals, and consequently as delivered in many Lodges, is open to serious objections. It is a marvellous composition, and is admirably adapted to the purpose for which it was intended, namely, to impress upon the minds of the newly Initiated Brethren 'the Excellence of our Institution and the qualifications' (the duties and the responsibilities) 'of its Members;' still, it is capable of improvement in some of its clauses. The author of this work has for many years delivered the Charge as follows.

It will be seen that for every change which has been introduced an explanation is given in a footnote, each of which should be read with care:

CHARGE.

Now that you have passed through the Ceremony of Initiation, allow me (on behalf of the Worshipful Master, and the Brethren of this Lodge)* to congratulate you on having become a Member of our Ancient and Honourable Fraternity.

* This only to be said if anyone other than the W. M. delivers the Charge.

Ancient it undoubtedly is, having subsisted from time immemorial, and Honourable it must be acknowledged to be, because by a natural tendency it conduces to render all those honourable, who are strictly obedient to its precepts. Indeed, no Institution can boast a more solid foundation than that upon which Freemasonry rests, namely, the practice of every moral and social virtue ; and to so high an eminence has its credit been advanced, that monarchs* in every age have been promoters of the art, have not thought it derogatory to their dignity to exchange the sceptre for the *gavel*, have patronised our mysteries, and have joined in our assemblies.

* In the Charge as it is usually given, this part of the sentence runs thus : ' that monarchs *themselves* have been promoters of the Art, have not thought it derogatory to their dignity to exchange the sceptre for the *trowel*, have patronised our mysteries, and *even* joined in our assemblies.' The words in italics, ' themselves ' and ' even,' imply an excess of condescension on the one side, and of humility on the other, that is most uncomplimentary to our Order. The implication is, ' they have stooped so low as *even* to come to the meetings of Lodges.' We may, and we do feel honoured by the Patronage of Royalty (as in the person of His Majesty), and by the presence of the scions of Royal Houses in our Lodges ; but we are not called upon to abase ourselves verbally in our allusions to our Royal Patrons or visitors.

The ' trowel ' is not one of our ' working tools.' No mention is made of it in either of the Ceremonies or of the Lectures. The ' gavel ' is not only one of our regular ' working tools,' and has a symbolical signification, but it is ' the emblem of Authority.' It is so designated when it is presented severally to the W. M. and to the Wardens on the day of Installation. This truly masonic working tool would naturally be placed in the hands of Royal Members of the Order (who always quickly attain to the W. M.'s chair), and this implement should be named in the Charge rather than the trowel. It is true the trowel is used by Royal Personages at the laying of a foundation-stone, but it is so used by all sorts and conditions of men—*or women*—who perform those functions.

As a Freemason, I would first recommend to your serious study the Volume of the Sacred Law, charging you to consider it as the unerring standard of truth and justice, and to regulate your actions by the Divine precepts which it contains; therein you will be taught the important duties you owe to God, to your neighbour, and to yourself.

To God, by never mentioning His name but with that awe and reverence which are due from the creature to his Creator, by imploring His aid upon all your lawful undertakings, and by looking up to Him in every emergency for comfort and support.

To your neighbour, by acting with him upon the Square, by rendering to him every kind office which justice or mercy may require, by soothing his afflictions, by relieving his necessities, and by doing unto him in all things as in similar cases you would wish that he should do unto you.

And to yourself, by such a prudent and well-regulated course of discipline as may best conduce to the preservation of your corporeal and mental faculties in their fullest energy, thereby enabling you to employ those talents wherewith God has blessed you, as well to His glory as to the welfare of your fellow-creatures.

As a Citizen of the World, I have next to enjoin you to be exemplary in the discharge of your Civil Duties, by never proposing or at all countenancing any act which may have a tendency to subvert the peace and good order of Society; by rendering due obedience to the laws of any state which may for a time become the place of your residence or may afford you its protection; and above all by an unwavering allegiance to the Sovereign of your Native Land, ever remembering that nature has implanted in the breast of man a sacred, and it should be an indissoluble attachment to the country from which he derives his birth and his infant nurture. As an Individual, I would further recommend to you the practice of every Domestic as well as public Virtue :* let Temperance chasten you, Fortitude support you, Prudence direct you, and Justice be the guide of all your actions; being at all times especially careful to maintain in unsullied brightness that truly Masonic Jewel† which has been already amply illustrated, namely, Charity.

Still, however, as a Freemason, there are other excellences of character to which your attention may be

* Here Temperance, Fortitude, Prudence, and Justice are placed in the order in which they occur in the sixth section of the First Lecture. It would be difficult to find a reason for placing them in a different order in the Charge.

† In the Charge as it is usually given these words occur, 'those truly Masonic *ornaments, Benevolence and Charity.* The word 'Charity,' in its true Scriptural and Masonic sense, comprises Benevolence (derived from *bene* and *volo*—' to wish well '), and Beneficence (from *bene* and *facio*—' to do well '—*i.e.*, to do good to others). Charity may, and where necessary and practicable always does, evince itself by the giving of alms or aids to the needy, the distressed, and the afflicted ; but the giving of alms does not constitute Charity. St. Paul (1 Cor. xiii. 3) writes thus : ' And though I bestow all my goods to feed the poor . . . and have not Charity, it profiteth me nothing.' A strong objection lies also against the use of the word ' ornaments' in this connection. ' The Ornaments of the Lodge' are clearly defined in the First Tracing Board. ' They are the Mosaic Pavement, the Indented or Tessellated Border, and the Blazing Star or Glory in the Centre,' whereas Charity is described in the First Lecture as ' the brightest *jewel* that adorns our Masonic profession.'

peculiarly and forcibly directed. Among the foremost of these are Secrecy, Fidelity, and Obedience. The Secrecy required of you is an inviolable adherence to the O... which you have entered into, never improperly to divulge any of those Masonic Secrets which have now been, or may hereafter be, communicated to you, and carefully to avoid all occasions which may inadvertently lead you to betray them.

Your Fidelity must be exemplified by a close conformity to the Constitutions of the Fraternity, by adhering to the Ancient Landmarks of the Order, by never attempting to extort or to otherwise improperly obtain the Secrets of a Superior Degree, and by refraining from recommending anyone to a participation in our Secrets, unless, from a previous knowledge of his character, you have good grounds for believing that by a fidelity equal to your own and by strict rectitude of life and actions he will ultimately reflect honour on our choice.

Your obedience must be proved by a strict observance of our Laws and Regulations, by a prompt attention to all Signs and Summonses, by a modest and correct demeanour in the Lodge, by abstaining, while there, from every topic of religious or political discussion, by a ready acquiescence in all Votes and Resolutions duly passed by a majority of the Brethren, and by a perfect submission to the will of the Master and his Wardens when acting in the discharge of the duties of their respective offices.

And as a last general recommendation, let me exhort you to dedicate yourself to such pursuits as may enable you to become at once respectable in life, useful to mankind, and an honour to the Fraternity of which you have this day been admitted a member. That you will more especially cultivate such of the Liberal Arts and Sciences as may lie within the compass of your attainment, and that, without neglecting the ordinary duties of your station in life, you will feel yourself called upon to make a daily advancement in Masonic Knowledge.

From the exemplary manner in which you have conducted yourself during the Ceremony of your Initiation, and from the very commendable attention you have given to this Charge, we are led to hope that you will duly appreciate the value of Freemasonry, and that there may be indelibly imprinted upon your heart the sacred principles of Truth, of Honour, and of Virtue. So mote it be.

H.—EXPLANATION OF THE WORKING TOOLS.

Those of the Second Degree Explained—An Illustration of the Explanation being Divided among the Three Principal Officers—Same Plan may be followed in First and Third Degrees.

H.—The Explanation of the Working Tools of the Second Degree is given here, according to the practice of some Lodges, in which (as has been mentioned in this work) the Worshipful Master, and the Senior and the Junior Warden, each explains the Implement which designates his Office, and in which the same course is followed in the First and the Third Degrees.

(*The Can. is conducted to the north, facing the J. W.*)

W. M.—You will now attend to an explanation of the Working Tools of a Fellow-Craft Freemason. They are the Square,

S. W.—The Level,

J. W.—And the Plumb-rule.

W. M. (*taking up Square*).—The Square is to try and adjust all rectangular corners of buildings, and to assist in bringing rude matter into due form.

S. W. (*takes up Level*).—The Level is to lay levels, and to prove horizontals.

J. W. (*takes up Plumb-rule*).—And the Plumb-rule is to adjust and prove all uprights, while fixing them upon their proper bases.

W. M.—But in this Degree, as well as in the First, we, not professing to be Operative but Free and Accepted or Speculative Masons, apply these Tools to our Morals. In this sense, the Square teaches us to regulate our lives and actions by the Masonic line and rule, and so to correct and order our conduct in this life as to render us acceptable to that Divine Being from Whom all goodness emanates, and to Whom we must give an undisguised account of our lives and actions.

S. W.—The Level demonstrates, that we are all sprung from the same stock, are partakers of the same nature, and sharers of the same hope ; and although distinctions among men may be highly necessary, in order to preserve due subordination, and to reward merit and ability, yet there is no eminence of station which should cause us to forget that we are all Brethren, and that he who is placed on the lowest spoke of Fortune's Wheel is equally entitled to our regard with him who has attained its highest round; for a time will most assuredly come—and the best and wisest of us know not how soon—when all distinctions, save those of Piety and Virtue, shall cease, and Death, the Great Destroyer, shall reduce us all to the same level.

J. W.—The Infallible Plumb-rule, which, like Jacob's Ladder, forms a line of union between Heaven and Earth, and is the criterion of Moral Rectitude and Truth, teaches us, that to walk with Humility and Uprightness before God, neither turning to the right hand nor to the left from the strict path of Virtue, is a duty incumbent upon every Freemason. Not to be an enthusiast, a persecutor, or a slanderer; or a reviler of Religion; neither inclining to avarice, injustice, nor malice; nor to the envy and contempt of our fellow-creatures, but giving up every selfish propensity which may tend to injure others, and to steer the Bark of Life over the rough Seas of Passion, without quitting the Helm of Rectitude, constitutes the highest degree of perfection to which human nature is capable of attaining. As the Builder raises his Column by the Level and the Perpendicular, so ought every Freemason to carry himself in this life; to observe a due medium between Avarice and Profusion, to hold the Scales of Justice with an equal Poise, to make every Passion and Prejudice coincide with the strict line of his Duty, and in every pursuit to have Eternity in view.

W. M.—Thus the Square teaches us Morality;

S. W.—The Level, Equality;

J. W.—And the Plumb-rule, Justice and Uprightness of life and actions.

W. M.—So that by Square conduct,

S. W.—Level steps,

J. W.—And Upright actions,

W. M.—We may hope to ascend to those ethereal* Mansions where the just will assuredly meet their reward.

I.—*Our* Grand Master as applied to H. A. B.

Since the publication of the previous edition of this book, a new edition of the ' Revised Ritual of Craft Masonry ' has been published. In it much new matter has been introduced in the notes (and the introductory remarks), well worthy of the attention of every serious student of the work of the craft. One note at the beginning of the Third Degree is of special interest and importance ; so it has been thought desirable to include it in the new edition of this book.

[Note.—In this edition of ' The Revised Ritual ' it will be noticed that throughout the Ceremony of Raising to the Third Degree the word ' our ' in connection with ' Grand Master ' as applied to H. A. B. is entirely omitted. One may well wonder how that word ever came to be so applied, and to ask how it can be possible that a man who died fully 2,900 years ago can be *our* Grand Master.

* The word ' Immortal ' is wrong as applied to ' Mansions.' Nothing can be immortal which has never had life. The word ' Eternal ' might be used, but ' Ethereal Mansion ' occurs in the Tracing Board of the First Degree ; thus—' figuratively speaking, an *ethereal* mansion, veiled from mortal eyes by the starry firmament.' The words ' whence all goodness emanates ' do not carry out the idea of the hope previously expressed to the same extent as the words given in the text appear to do.

In one of the higher Degrees it is stated that 'Solomon, King of Israel, Hiram, King of Tyre, and H. A. B., presided over the Second or Sacred Lodge.' In a still higher Degree these names are placed in the same order of sequence, followed by the words, 'the three Grand Masters who presided over the Second or Sacred Lodge.'

In each of these cases the names of S... K... I... and H... K... T... precede the name of H... A... B... From this it would appear that if one only of the three is to be adopted *for all time* as *our* Grand Master (in other words, as perpetual Grand Master of Freemasons throughout the world, and through all generations), then the preference should be given to King Solomon, as being the first, the highest, and immeasurably the greatest of the triumvirate.

The use (or rather the misuse) of the word in question is likely to be—and doubtless often is—a stumbling-block in the way of an educated and intelligent Brother who is taking the Third Degree. He will know that H.R.H. the Duke of Connaught (or, in the time to come, his successor) is *our* Grand Master, and he will surely wonder how a man who was engaged in the building of King Solomon's Temple nearly 3,000 years ago can possibly be *our* Grand Master. No valid reason can be given for the retention of the word, and in this enlightened age we ought carefully to avoid making, or retaining in our Ceremonies, any statement, or even a suggestion, of that which is contrary to reason, and which has no shadow of foundation in fact.

Throughout the following pages it will be found

that the title 'Grand Master,' as applied to H. A. B., is fully recognised. When the name is mentioned to the Candidate for the first time, it is given in these words, '...an ancient Grand Master of our Order H. A. B....' This gives to him his proper status in the events about to be narrated, and avoids the anachronism of claiming as *our* G. M. the very man, 'the manner of whose . . .' is about to be narrated to the Candidate.

In the remaining portion of the Ceremony, the word 'the' is substituted for 'our.' Good reason exists for the use of the word 'the' in this connection. H. A. B. was the one of the three Grand Masters who alone was personally connected with the events detailed in the narrative, the predominant figure in the scene about to be enacted ; he was, therefore, at that time—and is now—emphatically *the* Grand Master, whose ' untimely —— ' we commemorate in the Third Degree, and whom the Candidate is himself about to ' figuratively represent '* in the ensuing Ceremony.

In the following pages will be found an explanation of the meaning of the word ' A. B.' following the name H. It is barely possible that the candidate could ever have heard the name with that addition— *it is not in the Bible ;* and, hearing it then for the first time, he would naturally wonder who H. A. B. could possibly be. But given the explanation (on pages 104, 105), supported and authenticated as it is by Scripture references and quotations, the personality of

---

* The answer to one of 'the test questions in the Third Degree' runs thus : 'By having figuratively represented him when I was raised to the sublime Degree of a Master Mason.'

the man, and the whole subsequent narrative, will be made clear and intelligible.]

The passage to which allusion is made in the last paragraph runs thus :

It is here necessary that I should explain to you the meaning of the word A. B. which I just now used in connection with the name Hiram. It is a Hebrew word signifying the son of a widow. It is written in the volume of the Sacred Law that, in accordance with the request of King Solomon, Hiram, King of Tyre, sent to him a man who was well skilled in all details connected with 'the erection of stately and superb edifices,' to assist King Solomon in designing, erecting, beautifying, and adorning the Temple at Jerusalem. This man is described in the volume of the Sacred Law as 'the son of a widow woman of Tyre,' and his name, like that of the King of Tyre, was Hiram. These two ancient worthies—both bearing the same name, and both having been *at that time* (in conjunction with King Solomon) Grand Masters in our Order—are mentioned in various portions of the annals of Freemasonry, sometimes separately, some-times in juxtaposition ; and in order to distinguish be-tween the two, we call the one Hiram, King of Tyre, the other H. A. B.—that is, Hiram the son of the widow.

J.—Ornaments of the Lodge.

The Porch, the Dormer, the Square Pavement—No Foundation for them as part of K. S. T.—Remarks.

J.—'The Porch, the Dormer, and the Square Pave-ment.'

It is far better to omit all mention of these, the so-called 'Ornaments of a Master Mason's Lodge.'

There is not in the whole Bible the faintest shadow of foundation for supposing that they ever formed part of King Solomon's Temple. There is no room for doubt upon the subject; nothing can be more clear than the description given in the Bible of the whole internal arrangement of the Temple; and the references given in the following remarks will show how entirely the Scripture accounts differ from the description in the Third Ceremony.

There could have been no 'Porch' to the entrance to the Holy of Holies. The only Porch was outside, at the entrance to the Temple, on either side of which the Two Great Pillars stood. The 'Dormer' is a pure invention. No such thing is mentioned (see 1 Kings vi. and 2 Chron. iii.). None was needed. The High Priest alone, and he only once a year, entered the Holy of Holies; and the Shekinah was there, the visible manifestation of the Divine Presence in the Pillar of Cloud and of Fire. In Kings (vi. 30) it is distinctly stated 'the floor of the house he overlaid with gold within and without;' that is, in every part, and certainly the Holy of Holies would not be less richly floored than the rest; consequently, 'the square pavement' is an error. As a matter of course, the High Priest must walk upon the floor of the Holy of Holies, be it what it might, as he must go in at the door; but it would be absurd to say that the door was for the High Priest to enter by. The floor was just a necessary part of the structure, as were the walls and the ceiling, the whole being not simply or even primarily for the use of the High Priest, seeing that he entered it but once a year. The Holy of Holies was the receptacle for the Ark of the Covenant, and the Mercy Seat, with the Cherubim, etc. (see Exodus xxxvii.). Then it is stated in the ordinary ritual that the office of the High Priest was to burn incense once a year ; that is true, but he had many other things to do on the Great Day of Atonement (see Leviticus xvi.). He had to offer a young bullock and two kids ; then the Ceremony of the Scape-goat had to be gone through, and much in the way of ' Atonement.' The whole chapter is full of the various acts of ' Atonement,' but it has not one word to justify the assertion that the office of the High Priest on that day was ' to pray fervently that the Almighty...peace and tranquillity upon the Israelitish nation during the ensuing year.' He did nothing of the kind, as a perusal of Lev. xvi. will clearly show. It may be mentioned that the words ' peace and tranquillity ' are used twice in the Third Ceremony ; such a conjunction occurs nowhere in the Bible.

K.

THE ENTERED APPRENTICE'S SONG.

COME let us prepare ; We Brothers that are
   Here met on this happy occasion ;
We'll quaff and we'll sing ; Be he peasant* or King,
   Here's a health to an Accepted Mason.

  * One early version of this song has it, ' Be he *beggar* or King.' Peasant is preferable. In the first section of the first Lecture we read, ' Brother to a King, fellow to a Prince, and companion to a *peasant*, if a Freemason and found worthy.' Another version gives, ' Our wine has a spring.' This does not express the meaning of the verse, which is this : ' However exalted be his rank, or however lowly be his condition in life, if a man be a

The world tries in vain Our secrets to gain,
    And still let them wonder and guess on ;
They ne'er can divine A word or a sign
    Of a Free and an Accepted Mason.

'Tis this and 'tis that, They cannot tell what,
    Why the great men of every Nation,
Should aprons put on, And make themselves one
    With a Free and an Accepted Mason.

Great Kings, Dukes, and Lords Have laid by their swords,
    Our Myst'ries to put a good grace on ;
And have not been ashamed To hear themselves named
    As a Free and an Accepted Mason.

Antiquity's pride We have on our side,
    And we keep up our old reputation ;
There's nought but what's good To be understood
    By a Free and an Accepted Mason.

We're true and sincere, We're just to the Fair ;
    They'll trust us on any occasion ;
No mortal can more The Ladies adore
    Than a Free and an Accepted Mason.

(All rise and join hands.)

Then join hand in hand, To each other firm stand ;
    Let's be merry and put a bright face on :
No Order can boast So noble a toast
    As a Free and an Accepted Mason.

(Repeat.)

No Order can boast So noble a toast
    As a Free and an Accepted Mason.

Freemason we are equally ready to drink to his health.' The words, 'Let's drink, *laugh*, and sing,' in the older versions, have a Bacchanalian flavour which is objectionable, and the word 'laugh' is quite inappropriate.

Oxford Freemasons of say forty-five years ago, may have heard Brother Bossom, the stout porter of Brazenose, sing this song. For a considerable time he gave the last line of the first verse thus : ''ere's *an* 'ealth to an Accepted Mason.' This caused a laugh for a time, until it became too bad to bear, and one evening there was a simultaneous shout of ' Here's *a* health,' and this was continued until he substituted the 'a' for 'an,' but the two 'h's' were beyond his reach entirely.

L.—The Installation Ceremony.

A Work of the character of this treatise could hardly
be considered to be complete, if, after having dealt
somewhat freely with the Ceremonies of the three
Degrees, no mention were made of the Installation of
the Worshipful Master. The remarks, however, which
we have to make upon this Ceremony will apply
rather to Ritual than to Etiquette ; it seemed therefore
more desirable to discuss the subject in this place
than in the body of the work itself.

We will first consider the question of 'the opening
of a Board of Installed Masters.' We have here a
case which is a perfect parallel with that of 'Hearty
good wishes.' A rumour (it is nothing more) has got
abroad (or perhaps we may say has been industriously
circulated) that the Ceremonial opening of a Board
of Installed Masters has either been forbidden by, or
is in disfavour with Grand Lodge. *There is no valid
foundation for such a report ; the question has never been
brought before Grand Lodge, in any way, at any time*

One reason, or we may say excuse, for declaring the
Board of Installed Masters open, instead of opening it
in form, is that it saves time. How much time ?
Three or four minutes. The opening of the Lodge in

the First and the Third Degrees each takes longer than this, and yet one never hears a suggestion of the opening being done by declaration in either Degree ; and these are of monthly occurrence, while the Board of Installed Masters is opened once only in the year. There is, unfortunately, a growing tendency to cut short this, the most important function of the year. Why should this be? surely not that more time shall be devoted to the Banquet ! If so the remedy would be to call the Lodge together half an hour earlier. The time taken up by a *full* performance of the Ceremony, including the opening and closing of the Board of Installed Masters, would not exceed by half an hour the time occupied by a slipshod and perfunctory performance, with the Board of Installed Masters declared open.

The Installed Masters' is a Degree as much as are the Entered Apprentices', the Fellow-Crafts', the Master Masons', or the exalted Degree of the Royal Arch. It has its own particular Ceremony, by which alone a Master can be lawfully inducted into the Chair ; it has its own Obligations and its traditional history, its S...s, G..., and W.... It gives a distinct and honourable status in the Craft ; it raises its possessor high above the level of the ordinary Members of the Lodge, and it makes him a Ruler and Elder in the Order. It possesses every constituent element of a Degree, and it should no more be deprived of its ceremonial opening and closing than should any of the Degrees which precede or which follow it.

'The Revised Ritual' has the opening and closing of a Board of Installed Masters in full.

There is nothing in the least degree objectionable, nothing unconstitutional, in the Ceremony of opening and closing of a Board of Installed Masters. It is difficult to understand what ground of objection can be alleged against it. It would appear to be of ancient date ; it is in harmony with the spirit of the whole of the Ceremonies of the Craft ; and unless and until it is actually forbidden by a special enactment of Grand Lodge, Brethren are as free to use it as they are to use any other of the Ceremonies of Craft Masonry, notwithstanding any personal objection in any quarter.

A glance at some of the older Rituals (and even the more modern editions) will show great divergences in the Ceremony of the Installation of a Worshipful Master. The older copies are at one with regard to the Queen of Sheba, while the newer school have eliminated all mention of her visit to Jerusalem. Again, some of the older copies bring in H. A. B. This is clearly an anachronism. H. A. B. came by his untimely death '*before* the completion of King Solomon's Temple,' while the Queen of Sheba 'came to Jerusalem' after the completion of 'the house of the Lord, and the king's house.' See 1 Kings ix. verse 2 ; and 1 Kings x. verses 1 and 2.

If, instead of H. A. B., we substitute Adoniram (as in more recent editions), the difficulty is solved. In verse 4 of chapter x. the statement is clear that the Queen of Sheba had 'seen . . . the house that he had built'; the king would escort her there. At that time it is more than probable that a great number of persons would be present, and among them Adoniram,

who 'was over the Tribute.' Now, inasmuch as
Adoniram would be well known for his masterly skill,
in connection with the preparation in the Lebanon of
the wood and the stone used in the building of the
Temple, we may certainly conclude that 'King Solomon perceiving him standing modestly aside, and
wishing to confer upon him the especial honour of
presenting him to the queen,' would *beckon* him to
approach.

This is no fancy sketch or flight of imagination ; it
is a fair conclusion to be drawn from the Scripture
narrative ; it has inherent probability, founded upon a
sound substratum of Scriptural fact ; and it inter-
weaves our Masonic tradition of Adoniram with the
interesting episode of the visit of the Queen of Sheba
to Jerusalem, which is related in 1 Kings x., verses 1
to 9 inclusive—verses which for beauty of expression,
for power of graphic description, and for evidence of
inherent truthfulness, have few parallels in sacred or
secular history.

And what do the Brethren of the modern school,
who are so anxious to extirpate what one (at least) of
them calls 'the Queen of Sheba business,' offer us in
the place of our time-honoured tradition, with its
genuine Scriptural foundation ?   Nothing but a purely
imaginary account of 'the king and the princes of his
household going to view the buildings of the Temple'
(the Bible contains no mention of this), and that
during this visit the King beckoned to H. A. B. This
visit, therefore, must have occurred previously to the
completion of the Temple.

There can be no doubt that the King and those of

his household often went up to the Temple during the progress of the work, and they would upon those occasions certainly be attended by the Chief Architect. Then what was this special occasion which is selected as the *fons et origo* of the S... of an Installed Master? In explaining the Grand and Royal S... (or, as some have it, 'the S... of J. and E.'), precisely the same words are used: 'K. S. and the Princes of his household went to view it' (the completed building), when, as though it were a new revelation, instead of its having been familiar to them during its progress for seven years and more, they are said, 'with one simultaneous motion, to have exclaimed, "O wonderful Masons!"' Not a single verse can be found in the Bible giving the slightest shadow of evidence of any such visits, upon any occasion, by the King and the Princes. (What Princes?) These are pure inventions, meagre, uninteresting, and without the least show of even probability to recommend them.

The references in the Bible to Adoniram and his work are very brief, but they are highly significant. In 1 Kings v. 13, 14, we have the account of the levy of thirty thousand men, who were sent by Solomon to the Lebanon, 'ten thousand a month by courses.'...
'And Adoniram was over the levy.' In verse 18 of the same chapter we find, 'And Solomon's builders, and Hiram's builders, did hew *them*, and the stonesquarers; so they prepared *timber* and *stones* to build the house.' We have in a previous verse (9), 'My servants shall bring *them* down from Lebanon unto the sea: and I will convey them by sea in floats,' etc. In chapter vi., verse 7, it is stated, 'And the house, when

it was in building, was built of stone, made ready
before it was brought thither : so that there was
neither hammer, nor axe, nor any tool of iron heard
in the house while it was in building.'

Upon this solid Scriptural foundation our Masonic
tradition rests, which is briefly this, that, 'under the
strict personal superintendence of Adoniram, all the
materials, wood and stone, used in building of the
Temple were prepared in the Lebanon, and with such
marvellous accuracy of finish that, when they were
brought together at Jerusalem, each piece fitted to its
fellow with such exactness that the whole, when completed, appeared more like the work of T. G. A. O. T. U.
than of human hands.' *O si sic omnia !* Would that
all our traditions rested upon as firm a basis of Scriptural evidence as does this of Adoniram !

Many Installing Masters do substitute Adoniram
for H. A. B., in connection with either K. S. and
the Princes of his household, or with the Queen of
Sheba. A distinguished Deputy Provincial Grand
Master of a very large Province, a Grand Warden,
and a man eminent for ability and for untiring zeal in
the work of Freemasonry, when performing the ceremony of Installation (which he did in many Lodges
year after year), besides never omitting the Opening
and Closing of a Board of Installed Masters, always
brought in *Adoniram* and *the Queen of Sheba*, and in
addition he *read aloud* the first nine verses of
1 Kings x. previously to repeating the narrative of
the traditional history, culminating in Adoniram's
approaching his Royal Master and all that then
transpired. His rendering of the ceremony was, for

purity of diction, for dignity and grace in action, and for inspiring in all present a deep interest in the narrative, by far the best which in his long and varied experience the writer has ever seen ; it was clear and copious, 'without o'erflowing full,' compelling the rapt attention of his hearers, and calculated to produce a lasting effect for good upon those whom he installed. Again we may exclaim, ' *O si sic omnes !* He was no innovator; he would not have allowed in his Province the elimination of 'the Queen of Sheba *business*,' and to the end of his life he never, upon any occasion, omitted the ceremonial opening and closing of the Board of Installed Masters.

M.—Vocal Music in the Lodge.

In *The Freemason* of July 12th, 1890, the following paragraph appeared among the 'Masonic Notes':

'Bro. Lovegrove writes in reference to the correspondence that has appeared in our columns respecting music in Lodges, advising that a reference be made to the Grand Secretary as to whether hymn-singing is permissible at all.'

The author of this work wrote a letter upon the subject, which was inserted in *The Freemason* of July 26th, 1890. In it he stated that there was no need to trouble the Grand Secretary upon the subject; that he had been present at the Consecration of the

Centurion Lodge at Manchester on November 15th, 1889, when the Grand Secretary himself performed the Ceremony, assisted by the Very Worshipful Brothers Philbrick and Fenn, and other members of Grand Lodge ; that during the Ceremony two hymns, three anthems, and six responses were sung ; and that, after this example of a musical Masonic service, performed in the presence and under the authority of the Grand Secretary, Brethren need have no doubt or misgiving as to 'hymn-singing being permissible' during Masonic ceremonies, 'because, if it be right and proper during the Consecration of a Lodge, it is equally right as accompanying any and all of the Ceremonies of the Lodge.'

Some paragraphs may here be given verbatim from the letter itself :

' My memory extends to over sixty years in Freemasonry ; during this long period of time I have visited Lodges in many different Provinces in England, and I have heard—times without number—" Psalms and Hymns and Spiritual Songs " during the several Ceremonies, and to my knowledge the " permissibility " of the practice has never before been questioned. . . .'

' Bro. W. M. Spark, the composer and compiler of the " Freemason's Liber Musicus," could have had no doubt as to the perfect propriety of vocal as well as of instrumental music, as accompaniments of our Ceremonies. The practice is old, *to my knowledge ;* it is truly reverential and devotional ; the hymns, etc., are well selected and appropriate ; they add materially to the solemnity and the impressiveness of the several

Ceremonies ; and last, and not least, they afford to the whole of the Brethren present the opportunity of joining—as they do generally—with heart and voice in those compositions. . . .'

'One hears occasionally of some action, "It was worse than a crime—it was a blunder." This exactly describes that which would be the general feeling among the Members of our Order generally, if any authoritative pronouncement were made adverse to the good old custom of "Hymn-singing" during Masonic Ceremonies.'

We may here repeat that ' no man or body of men ' can rightly claim authority to alter or to abrogate an old-established custom of our Order, except the Grand Lodge itself, and then only after due notice of motion shall have been given ; and that any change from the established customs of the Craft made by Grand Lodge should be duly notified to every Lodge.

If the Brethren generally would recognise these facts, they would cease to give credence to and to assist in circulating baseless rumours to the effect that 'Grand Lodge' disapproves of this or that or the other custom of the Craft, and as to which subjects Grand Lodge has never expressed an opinion in any way.

Masonic Mourning.

In the event of the death of any high dignitary in the Craft, an order is sent by the Grand Secretary to each Lodge that mourning shall be worn by every brother for a certain period of time. In the case of a similar loss in a Province or District, the Provincial or District Grand Secretary would send a like order to every Lodge in his Province or District.

The regulation form of mourning dictated on these occasions is as follows : For Officers present and past of Grand Lodge, or of Provincial or District Grand Lodges, and for Officers of private Lodges, a black crape Rosette near the point of the collar above the jewel ; and for all Master Masons, Officers included, a similar crape Rosette just above the point of the flap of the Apron, and one on each of the lower corners, well clear of the bottom and the two sides.

For Fellow-Crafts and Entered Apprentices, two black crape Rosettes, one on each corner of the bottom edge of the Apron.

Black or white ties, and white, or, *preferably*, gray gloves, with black stitchings, should be worn. In either case uniformity is much to be desired ; on this point an expression of the wish of the Worshipful Master may be added to each circular. If it be thought necessary or desirable that the Lodge-room should be put into mourning, the following plan or any portion thereof may be adopted :

Each of the three pedestals may have a black cloth cover to fit the top, with a fall round the front and

18

the two sides eight inches deep, with a black bullion fringe of five inches round the lower edge.

The Master's and the two Warden's chairs may have a cap of black cloth fitted to the shape of the top of the back of each chair, about twelve inches deep, fringed on the lower edge the same as the covers on the pedestals. The three candlesticks and the columns should each have a trimming of crape, so also should the Deacons' wands.

If the Banner of the Lodge be displayed, it should have a large black crape Rosette on or near the top of the staff, and one of the same size (or nearly) on each of the four corners. If there be cords and tassels, they may be trimmed with crape.

If the occasion justify any further demonstration of mourning, advantage may be taken of any salient portion of the room and the furniture, such as the tops of windows and doors, and the Secretary's table, the organ or harmonium, upon which crape or cloth may be placed Much may depend upon the occasion of the mourning, whether it be for a high dignitary in the Craft (as previously mentioned), or for one of the then Principal Officers, or a Past Master of the Lodge.

In the case of the death of an ordinary member, it is unusual for the Lodge to go into mourning ; a letter of condolence to the family of the deceased, signed by the Master and the Wardens, is generally considered to be sufficient. This mark of respect should not by any means be omitted.

INDEX.

THE END,

BILLING AND SONS, LTD., PRINTERS, GUILDFORD.

Foolscap 8vo., 256 pages, cloth, price 4s. 6d. net, post free.

A CONCISE CYCLOPÆDIA OF FREEMASONRY;

OR,

Handbook of Masonic Reference.

COMPILED FROM VARIOUS SOURCES BY

E. L. HAWKINS, M.A. Oxon,

Junior Steward Quatuor Coronati Lodge, No. 2076;
P.M. Nos. 357, 478, & 1842; P. Prov. S.G.W. & P.
Prov. G. Sec. of Oxfordshire; P.Z. 357; P. Prov.
G.S.E. of Oxfordshire; 30° (A. & A. Rite); P.S.
Chapter 40; P. Prov. G. Swd.-Bearer (Mark), Berks
& Oxon; K.T.; K M.; Author of "A History of
Freemasonry in Oxfordshire."

THE object of the "Concise Cyclopædia of Freemasonry" is to furnish brief yet lucid answers
to the questions which occur to the mind of the
ordinary Freemason, who has neither time nor
inclination to embark upon a regular study of
Masonic History and Antiquities. . . . The compiler's idea has been to present only the *facts* of
Masonic History, leaving *theories* and abstruse disquisitions to the writers of more pretentious works.

———————

A. LEWIS, 13, PATERNOSTER ROW, LONDON, E.C.

Τhe **Revised Ritual of Craft Freemasonry**. Including the Lectures, Installation Ceremony, etc., complete. Together with full Explanatory and Critical Notes and Scripture References. By an Old Past Master. Incorporating suggestions from several distinguished Past Masters. Price 9s. net, post free.

Second Edition, Revised, with Additional Notes and Instructions.

EXTRACTS FROM THE PREFACE.

' No thoughtful member of the Craft will doubt or deny that there is this much in the Ritual which requires correction, and a critical examination will show that many portions require to be recast in their phraseology. In this Ritual, wherever an alteration from the common forms of expression has been made, great care has been taken to preserve the full meaning and intention of the several passages, and good reasons will be found in the notes for every such alteration and correction. . . .

' No valid reason can be urged against the correction of proved errors, or against bringing the wording of our ceremonies into accordance with the text of the Bible, with the rules of grammar, with the common-sense meaning of the various sentences, and with the enlightenment of the age in which we live. . . .

' It is not to be expected, nor is it perhaps to be desired, that the ceremonies as they are here given should be adopted in their entirety. The best that can be hoped for is, that the attention of Brethren will be directed to the numerous errors which are pointed out, and *clearly proved*, in this Ritual '

In a paper written by the Very Worshipful Brother Whymper, Past Deputy District Grand Master of the Punjaub, and read at the meeting of that District Grand Lodge in 1889 upon the subject of Masonic Rituals, the following sentence occurs :

' To students of Rituals I commend " The Revised Ritual, by an Old Past Master," published last year. *The notes therein are of the highest possible value.*'

Brother Whymper was himself a writer of no mean eminence. His ' Religion of Freemasonry ' is an admirable composition.

LONDON: A. LEWIS, 13, PATERNOSTER ROW, E.C.

THIRD EDITION.

40 *pp.*, *Crown 8vo.*, *price* 1s. 6d. *net*, *post free.*

LODGE AND CHAPTER MUSIC.

CONTENTS:

I. THE CRAFT DEGREES.

AFTER EVERY PRAYER.
OPENING HYMN.
CLOSING HYMN.
NOTHING NOW REMAINS, ETC.
  CEREMONY—1st DEGREE.
ADMISSION.
1ST PERAMBULATION.
ADVANCING TO E.
SALUTING V. S. L.
RESTORATION.
TRIAL AND PROBATION.
INVESTITURE.
CHARITY.
RETIRING.
RE-ADMISSION.
  CEREMONY—2nd DEGREE.
ADMISSION.
1ST PERAMBULATION.
2ND PERAMBULATION.

ADVANCING TO E.
SALUTING V. S. L.
TRIAL AND PROBATION.
INVESTITURE.
RETIRING.
RE-ADMISSION.
  CEREMONY—3rd DEGREE.
ADMISSION.
PERAMBULATIONS.
ADVANCING TO E.
SALUTING V. S. L.
HEAVY MAUL.
REUNION.
TRIAL AND PROBATION.
INVESTITURE.
RETIRING.
RE-ADMISSION.
E. A. SONG.
WE MEET UPON THE LEVEL.

II. INSTALLATION OF THE WORSHIPFUL MASTER, Etc.

AFTER I. M. TAKES CHAIR.
AFTER THE O.B.
PROCESSIONAL ODE.

1ST, 2ND, AND 3RD PERAMBU-
  LATIONS.
AFTER CONCLUDING ADDRESS.

MASONIC FUNERAL CEREMONY.

III. ROYAL ARCH CHAPTER.

OPENING CHAPTER.
CLOSING CHAPTER.
NOTHING NOW REMAINS, ETC.
ENTRANCE OF CANDIDATE.
AFTER ANSWER TO QUESTION.

AFTER CAN. HAS BEEN R. TO L.
ENTRANCE OF THREE M.MS.
M.MS. FURNISHED WITH IMPS.
BEFORE THE ADDRESS.
AFTER THIRD LECTURE.

A. LEWIS, 13, PATERNOSTER ROW, LONDON, E.C.

Fourth Edition, medium 16mo., 64 pages, in coloured wrapper, price 1s. net, post free.

FREEMASONRY: Its History, Principles, and Objects. With an Introduction by Bro. the Rev. JOHN T. LAWRENCE, M.A. (Oxon.), Author of " Masonic Jurisprudence and Symbolism " (on Progress, Appreciation, and Safeguards).

" We most cordially recommend this little work to the serious perusal not only of those who are already numbered amongst the Craft, but also of all who may meditate on entering the ranks of Freemasonry. It is a *vade mecum* of very convenient form, and although consisting of only fifty-six pages, the amount of Masonic lore therein contained is really astonishing."—*Sunday Times.*

Pocket size, cloth, gilt edges price 2 . each net, post free.

MASONIC DIRECTORIES. A Series of Handbooks of Practical Directions for the Efficient Conduct of the Work throughout the Craft, Mark, and Royal Arch Degrees. By K. R. H. MACKENZIE, IX° (" Cryptonymus "), Author of " The Royal Masonic Cyclopædia," etc.

I.—The Deacon's Work (*Second Edition*).

II.—The Warden's Work (*Second Edition*).

III.—The Secretary's and Treasurer's Work.

IV.—The W. Master's Work (*Second Edition*).

V.—The Mark Work.

VI.—The Royal Arch Work.

These Volumes form a graduated school of Practical Masonic Instruction, and there are no other works in the English language presenting similar directions for general use.

A. LEWIS, 13, PATERNOSTER ROW, LONDON, E.C.

Foolscap 8vo., 360 pp., price 4s. 6d. net, post free.

MASONIC JURISPRUDENCE AND SYMBOLISM

As Interpreted by Grand Lodge Decisions.

By Bro. the Rev. JOHN T. LAWRENCE, M.A. Oxon, Past District G. Warden, Madras (Craft and Mark); Past Prov. G. Chaplain, East Lancs; P.Z., Past District G. Soj., P.E.P., etc. ; formerly Editor *Indian Masonic Review*.

With an INTRODUCTION by V. W. Bro. Canon HORSLEY, Past Grand Chaplain of England ; P.M. Quatuor Coronati Lodge.

PART I.

PART II.

A SERIES OF DIGESTS, WITH EXPLANATORY NOTES AND REFERENCES TO THE CONSTITUTIONS INVOLVED, OF ALL THE MORE IMPORTANT APPEALS DETERMINED BY GRAND LODGE SINCE 1867, WITH A NUMBER OF NOTABLE RULINGS BY DELEGATED AUTHORITIES.

A. LEWIS, 13, PATERNOSTER ROW, LONDON, E.C.